The Canadian Commission
A RECORD OF GOD'S UNFAILING FAITHFULNESS

By Victor Maxwell

THE CANADIAN COMMISSION

A RECORD OF GOD'S FAITHFULNESS

VICTOR MAXWELL

Belleville, Ontario, Canada

THE CANADIAN COMMISSION
Copyright © 2017, The Faith Mission (in Canada)

All Rights Reserved. No part of this publication may be reproduced, stored in a retrieval system or transmitted in any form or by any means—electronic, mechanical, photocopy, recording or any other— except for brief quotations in printed reviews, without the prior permission of the Mission.

All Scripture quotations, unless otherwise specified, are from *The Holy Bible, King James Version.* Copyright © 1977, 1984, Thomas Nelson Inc., Publishers.
• Scriptures marked NIV are from *The Holy Bible, New International Version.* Copyright © 1973, 1978, 1984, 2011 International Bible Society. Used by permission of Zondervan Publishing House. All rights reserved.

ISBN: 978-1-4600-0859-1
LSI Edition: 978-1-4600-0860-7
E-book ISBN: 978-1-4600-0861-4
(E-book available from the Kindle Store, KOBO and the iBooks Store)

To order additional copies, visit:
www.essencebookstore.com
www.faithmissioncanada.org

For more information, please contact:
The Faith Mission (in Canada)
10463 2nd Line, Campbellville, Ontario, L0P 1B0
Phone: 1-(905)-854-3284
Email: faithmissionoffice@gmail.com

Guardian Books is an imprint of *Essence Publishing,* a Christian Book Publisher dedicated to furthering the work of Christ through the written word. For more information, contact:
20 Hanna Court, Belleville, Ontario, Canada K8P 5J2
Phone: 1-800-238-6376 • Fax: (613) 962-3055
Email: info@essence-publishing.com
Web site: www.essence-publishing.com

CONTENTS

Preface 7
Commendations and Greetings 9
Introduction 15

Chapter 1 A Canadian Helps a Highlander 17
Chapter 2 How It All Began 23
Chapter 3 Crisis and Constraint 29
Chapter 4 The Faith Mission Begins 35
Chapter 5 Gospel Growth in Scotland 41
Chapter 6 Departures and Arrivals 47
Chapter 7 Welcome to Canada 53
Chapter 8 Abounding in the Work 59
Chapter 9 Ontario Outreach 65
Chapter 10 Passing the Baton 71
Chapter 11 Northlands 77
Chapter 12 British Columbia 83
Chapter 13 Maritime Ministry 93
Chapter 14 Nova Scotia Blessings 99
Chapter 15 Canadian Challenge Today 107
Chapter 16 No Secret What God Can Do 113
Chapter 17 Multi Ministries 121
Chapter 18 Abounding in the Work of the Lord 131

Chapter 19 How God Provides 137
Chapter 20 Praise and Testimonies 149
Chapter 21 Ladies' Spiritual Enrichment Retreat.....................167
Chapter 22 Kids' Clubs and Camps 177
Chapter 23 On Others' Shoulders 181
Chapter 24 April's Hope.......................................185
Chapter 25 Table Talk 189
Chapter 26 Ready for Anything 199
Chapter 27 On the Move......................................205
Chapter 28 Christ Alone 209
Chapter 29 Growing up and Going Out.....................217
Chapter 30 Parental Channels.................................221
Chapter 31 Their Labour of Love..............................225
Chapter 32 I Met the Saviour..................................231
Chapter 33 A Heart Cry for Revival...........................239
Chapter 34 Prayer, Evangelism, and Revival.................243
Chapter 35 The Great Commission 251

PREFACE

It is a challenge to pass a ministry from one generation to another. There are some simple reasons for this. The first generation of leaders had received their vision from God and courageously pioneered through hardships and the anguish of giving birth to their vision. The second generation is that of people heavily influenced by the founders; they receive their policies and follow their procedures, but have not necessarily wrestled with God in the same way the founders have. The third generation may easily follow the procedures but become distant from the deep, personal experience of God that gave birth to the mission. Hence ministries die. Leadership is replaced by management, and too often the church is littered with spiritually failing ministries and the tombstones of those long burned out.

The Faith Mission (in Canada) has risen to the challenge and kept hold of its heartbeat, core, and main vision through successive generations for the past ninety years. Like so many "unsung" ministries, the repercussions of their work for that period of time cannot be measured, but is widespread and rich.

This book is more than a narrative of these past ninety years, it is a challenge and stimulation to consider the quality of our own relationship with God and our own experience of the resources available to us—found in an encounter with the fullness of God to which the Faith Mission persistently points.

CHARLES PRICE
Minister at Large, The Peoples Church, Toronto

Commendations and Greetings

Researching material for this book has been both a blessing and a challenge. My heart has been stirred to cry out to God for a fresh outpouring of His Spirit both on the Faith Mission (in Canada) and the Church as a whole. In the early days of the Mission, souls were being saved in large numbers; these days it is more like a trickle.

Has sin become more sinful? Is the Devil more powerful? Are the promises of God less trustworthy? Has the Holy Spirit been withdrawn? Has God changed? I am glad to shout a resounding "NO" to all of these questions.

What then can we do? Let us take to heart the words that transformed D.L. Moody's life: "The world has yet to see what God can do through a man/woman wholly yielded to Him."

May the reading of this book challenge us all to a life of full surrender, holiness, obedience, prayer, and evangelism so that this generation may be reached with the Gospel and God's name glorified.

JOHN BENNETT
General Director, The Faith Mission (in Canada)

* * * * *

On behalf of the Board of the Faith Mission (in Canada) I want to express our praise and gratitude to God who has so richly blessed and provided for this missionary outreach during the past ninety years.

We extend our thanks to Victor Maxwell for using his writing skills to correlate numerous reports, pieces of information, and personal stories into this book.

We are deeply indebted to the early pioneering pilgrim ladies who laid the groundwork for our Mission away back in 1927. And we are equally grateful for the many who have continued to work throughout the years until the present day.

Thanks also goes to the many faithful prayerful people, without whose support our Mission would not have continued to exist for ninety fruitful years. God alone knows how great has been their contribution.

Canada is a massive and diverse landscape. The Mission's footprint is small, but what has been achieved by God's grace is truly remarkable.

Our prayer is that we will, in the years ahead, occupy every province and continue with John George Govan's desire to be a soul-winning agency for the glory of God.

In His service,

EDWIN HOEY
President, The Faith Mission (in Canada)

* * * * *

I first heard of the Faith Mission (in Canada) when I was a student at the Faith Mission Bible College, Edinburgh, Scotland in the mid-1970s. In fact, at that time I wondered whether the Lord might be directing me to serve with the Faith Mission (in Canada), but that was not to be. I have, however, held an interest in the work in that great land ever since.

Perhaps, for that reason, I have found it extremely interesting to read the draft of this book and have been deeply challenged that the founding principles of the Faith Mission in total dependence on God, selfless service for Him, and prevailing prayer continue to govern and guide this work. It is thrilling to read of how God has broken into lives, families, and on numerous occasions, whole communities in answer to prayer and the sacrificial service of those who have given themselves to this ministry.

Encouraging though it may be to reflect on past blessing, we must resist the temptation to rest on the laurels of the past. This heritage must spur us on, like those who have gone before, to rise to the challenge of making Christ known to the people of our generation. We must prevail at the throne of grace until God in His goodness visits our lives and lands again in a mighty move of revival.

God still answers the fervent effectual prayer of righteous men and women and is still able to meet the deepest needs of the people today. He is still able to transform whole communities as men, women, and children are convicted of their sins, repent and turn to Christ for forgiveness. Strategies and programs will accomplish little of eternal value unless we experience a real visitation from God as our forebears were privileged to see. Oh, that the challenge of revival would increasingly grip our hearts today.

May God lead, empower, and greatly use the workers of the Faith Mission (in Canada) as they move forward into the next era of making Christ known to the people of Canada.

JOHN TOWNEND
General Director, The Faith Mission (UK and Ireland)

* * * * *

For many years it has been my privilege to be associated with the Faith Mission (in Britain and in Canada). I have crossed the Atlantic on several occasions since 1983 to minister at Faith Mission events in Canada.

Fellowship with the Mission's leaders and workers on these visits has been very precious, and I have always been impressed with the spiritual calibre of all the personnel.

I am delighted that this account of ninety years of the Faith Mission (in Canada) is now available, and I commend it to all, praying that the reading of this volume will stir our hearts and move us all to seek God for a mighty spiritual awakening in Canada.

REV. TOM SHAW
Former President, The Faith Mission UK

It is written in Daniel 11:32, *"The people who know their God shall be strong and carry out great exploits."* You hold in your hand a remarkable record of a long line of God's heroes, for this exciting story of the Faith Mission, established in Scotland in 1886 and now celebrating ninety years of Gospel ministry in Canada.

Daniel's one-line evaluation of those believers who accomplish notable deeds for God is applicable to the workers of the Mission, for it gives us the threefold secret of their faithfulness and fruitfulness. Such people know their God, and in the pages of this book you will meet people who knew not just information about God, but intimacy with God; who became strong in the grace that is in Christ Jesus; and who carried out great exploits for their Lord.

This God-ordained sequence—intimacy, dynamic, and accomplishment—is illustrated again and again in the lives and ministry of those who are introduced in this book. Read it prayerfully, asking God to speak to you about becoming personally involved in prayer, evangelism, and revival. Join the Company of the Committed today.

TED RENDALL
Chancellor Emeritus, Prairie Bible Institute, Three Hills, Alberta
Professor of Preaching, The Stephen Olford Centre, Memphis, Tennessee

Commendations and Greetings

* * * * *

What a gracious gift God gave to Canada in sending the Faith Mission Pilgrims to our shores beginning in 1927. Through these past ninety years, their Gospel witness has been used by the Holy Spirit to draw thousands of children, youth, and adults into a transforming faith in Christ.

The burden of the Faith Mission for prayer, revival, and evangelism is the same vision that brought my wife Adrienne and me to Canada in 1961 to join with Canadian evangelist Ken Campbell. During the next seventeen years, we conducted about five hundred revival and evangelistic campaigns. In some of those outreaches, we were blessed to have workers with the Faith Mission, such as Hugh and Anne Jamieson, participating with us.

I'll never forget in 1964 attending an afternoon meeting with Ken in Toronto where Duncan Campbell was speaking. After the meeting that saintly man invited us to his room for further discussion and prayer. How our hearts burned within us as he opened his heart for revival.

In 1978 I became a pastor at Benton Street Baptist Church in Kitchener, Ontario, where we have enjoyed a hearty partnership with the Faith Mission for many years. Hester Dougan and others have ministered in several of our Daily Vacation Bible Schools. John and Isabel Bennett and team have led us for many years in annual prayer rallies. Some of our dear saints have hosted regular prayer meetings in their homes for the ministries of the Faith Mission.

It has been my joy to team with these Faith Mission workers in prayer gatherings, at rallies with Faith Mission Men, and in many events at the Faith Mission Conference Centre in Campbellville. May the Spirit-filled ministries of the Faith Mission (in Canada) during these past ninety years continue unabated to bear eternal fruit until our Lord Jesus returns for His Bride!

JIM REESE
Former Pastor, Benton Street Baptist Church, Kitchener, Ontario

* * * * *

"Remember those…who have spoken the word of God to you, whose faith follow, considering the outcome of their conduct. Jesus Christ is the same yesterday, today, and forever" (Hebrews 13:7,8 NKJV).

Throughout my fifty-plus years of living, God has blessed me on many occasions through His servants who serve in the Faith Mission. This book traces the faithfulness of God and the obedience of many men and women whose Spirit-led ministries have impacted Canada since 1927.

Read these accounts and rejoice in the marvellous guidance of God. Let your heart be stirred with accounts of Gospel proclamation across this nation. Though the names of these pilgrims may not be as familiar to you as they are to my family, you will find God stirring you to a greater diligence, a more fervent spirit, and lifelong service of Jesus, who is called the Christ!

REV. KEITH M. EDWARDS
Former Pastor, Thornloe Crossroads Baptist Church
Director of Church Initiatives & Internships, Heritage College & Seminary

Introduction

Sir Leonard Tilley, one of the Fathers of the Confederation of Canada and former Provincial Secretary for New Brunswick, suggested the name "Dominion of Canada" for the union of the four colonies of Nova Scotia, New Brunswick, Ontario, and Quebec. His suggestion was prompted after reading Psalm 72 the previous evening. Verse 8 struck him forcefully: *"He shall have dominion also from sea to sea, and from the river unto the ends of the earth."* On the basis of this Bible verse, Sir Leonard proposed the name "Dominion of Canada," and it was accepted by all the Founding Fathers of the great Confederation.

On July 1, 1867, the Dominion of Canada was born. The words from the Latin Vulgate Version of Psalm 72:8 are emblazoned on the coat of arms of Canada: *"a mari usque ad mare"*—"from sea to sea."

Five years before the founding of the Dominion of Canada, John George Govan was born in Glasgow, Scotland. He forsook his early and lucrative success in the business world to step out by faith to serve God. That step resulted in the founding of the Faith Mission in 1886 with its aim to seek first the Kingdom of God. In the succeeding years, his zealous ministry and that of hundreds of dedicated Faith Mission workers brought blessings, salvation, deepening of the Christian life, and the stirrings of revival all over the British Isles.

Canada, this "vast and vigorous land," which drew so many sturdy settlers of English, Irish, and Scottish extraction, became the sphere of service for the Blood-bought rights of King Jesus and our great Saviour when two Faith Mission Pilgrims arrived in Montreal in 1927.

From its simple beginnings in the city of Toronto, Ontario, the Faith Mission (in Canada) has established and maintained a glorious testimony for ninety years, to seek first the Kingdom of God throughout this great land. Through thick and thin, through evil report and good, this valiant band of Faith Mission workers has pioneered in frontier and settlement in an effort to break through the hardness of a country that has never experienced a nationwide revival. However, a gradual prayer consciousness began to take hold on individuals here and there across the nation as the years went by.

In 1964, Rev. Duncan Campbell from Scotland made his first visit to Toronto. When he spoke of the "Lewis Awakening," that mighty work of God in the Hebrides in Scotland, many hearts in Canada were stirred. Listening to the man of God who was so mightily used in that movement of the Spirit created an intense desire for a similar revival. "Do it again, Lord," was the inarticulate cry from burdened hearts. "This time let it be in Canada."

That is still our earnest prayer.

CHAPTER 1

A Canadian Helps a Highlander

Duncan Campbell was a sturdy Scottish Highlander who was born into a rugged crofting family in Benderloch, Western Scotland. With the outbreak of the Great War in 1914, Duncan's older brother, John, was conscripted to serve his country in the British Army. Two years later, midway through World War I, Duncan voluntarily enlisted in the Argyll and Sutherland Highlanders. He was soon drafted as a rookie machine-gunner to the battlefront in Belgium during the bloody and prolonged Flanders Campaign.

The atrocities and carnage of the war took hold on the young soldier. Many comrades lost their lives, limbs, or sight. Young Duncan was not only distressed by the senseless slaughter and cruelty that surrounded him; he was also struck by the brevity of life and the folly of young men neglecting their souls and being unprepared for death and eternity. These serious concerns were deeply etched upon his mind at the front line. He had seen scores of casualties among his colleagues, and many surviving soldiers asked Duncan to pray for them. They recognized the tall Highlander as a man of God.

After months of little progress on the Western Front, the Allied forces were subjected to a barrage during a concerted enemy assault. Their line suffered heavy losses and had to retreat from the vantage point they had occupied. In the commander's strategy to retake the ridge they had lost, Duncan was recruited to a Cavalry Division. He was detailed to be part of one of the last major cavalry charges at Amiens in April, 1918.

Mounted on his galloping horse, Duncan bravely rode across the fields into the fray of battle. He and his colleagues were soon overwhelmed by the enemy's force. Within minutes of the charge, Duncan and his horse were shot. The animal collapsed immediately, throwing the young Highlander into the mud and mire. He lay there severely wounded in the swamp that was no-man's land. The scene was horrendous with the dead, gore, and dying all around him. Wild, terrified, and riderless horses ran amok among them, sometimes trampling on the lifeless corpses of the dead or inflicting further lacerations on the injured.

As blood flowed from Duncan's open wounds, he was sure he was dying. He felt unworthy, but was glad he had trusted in Jesus Christ years earlier. Contemplating his impending meeting with the Saviour, he was grieved that he had accomplished so little in life.

Just then a second charge of the Canadian Horse Cavalry surged across the gory and muddy battlefield. As one Canadian line raced by, a horse's hoof struck Duncan on the spine. He cried out and helplessly writhed in pain. Those groans saved his life.

The Canadians had cleared the enemy line, and during a brief lull in the hostilities, the soldier whose horse had injured Duncan remembered the groan of an injured soldier and returned to where he lay. He dismounted from his horse, picked up the wounded Highlander, lifted him across his saddle, and galloped to the nearest Casualty Clearing Station.

This phase of the war soon led to the famous Battle of Amiens, which started three months later and proved to be the most deci-

Chapter 1—A Canadian Helps a Highlander

sive battle against the Germans on the Western Front. The German Army had been considerably strengthened by tens of thousands of troops who had been moved from the Eastern Front to the Western after Russia pulled out of the war. It took a coordinated attack by Allied artillery, tanks, infantry, and aircraft to eventually overcome the enemy. This enormous counter attack led to Germany's defeat and the end of the Great War.

The loss of blood had severely weakened Duncan, and it seemed death was near. As he lay across the Canadian soldier's saddle, he was still concerned how little he had accomplished as a Christian. Even in his weakness and near unconsciousness, he prayed the words of Robert Murray McCheyne, "Lord, make me as holy as a saved sinner can be."

Instantly the power of God filled and possessed him. The Holy Spirit swept through his being like a refining and cleansing flame, purging him until he felt as pure as an angel. Duncan sensed that God was so near to him that he was sure he was about to be ushered into Heaven, but this was not Heaven, not yet. God had more work for Duncan to do on earth.

This invigorating experience was a divine visitation to prepare the Scotsman for future days. Afterward, Duncan referred to that spiritual and pivotal experience in many different terms, but he was more concerned with the practical outworking of this personal revival rather than any theological labels.

The outcome of that reviving touch on his soul and body on that battlefield marked the rest of Duncan Campbell's life and ministry. That personal revival deepened this soldier's thirst for God, and consequently, he made a commitment to be an instrument that the Spirit of God could use anywhere and at anytime.

In 1964, Duncan Campbell visited Toronto, and in the first meetings, he related his story of his indebtedness to Canada and an unknown Canadian soldier whom God had used to spare his life—and what a life that was.

Decades before this, when Duncan Campbell was a teenager, the skirl of the bagpipes fascinated the young man. He quickly acquired a chanter, and within a short time, he became a proficient player of the bagpipes. The young and skilled Highlander earned the name "Am Plobaire Ruah"—"the Red Piper"—and was in high demand to entertain the crowds at many Highland concerts. Clad in kilt and sporran, bonnet and ribbons, his belt and buckles shone as he stood tall to play many familiar and favourite Scottish airs while scores of people, young and old, danced their Scottish reels around the floor.

It was while he was playing at one of these concerts that Duncan was struck with a deep sense of guilt and desolation. With difficulty, he excused himself from the company and withdrew from the gaiety of the concert that night. Friends tried to persuade him to stay, but the Holy Spirit had gripped Duncan's heart, and he could not resist. "I'm going home to get right with God," he announced to one of his friends.

During the three-mile walk home, carrying his pipes and swords, Duncan experienced a battle raging in his heart between the right and the wrong, Christ versus the world, to follow God's way or persist in his own way. In his heart, he knew he must decide. The hour was late, but as Duncan turned a corner near his home, he noticed a light in the small Memorial Hall where he had attended Sunday school years earlier. Curiosity compelled him to investigate why a light should be burning so late. As he drew nearer, he could hear someone's voice passionately praying. Cocking his ear to the keyhole, the Red Piper was startled to discover the voice was that of his father, passionately praying for his eldest son, Duncan.

Chapter 1—A Canadian Helps a Highlander

Duncan left his bagpiping paraphernalia outside and quietly slipped into the hall to sit beside his dad. On the platform, he saw two strange girls wearing peculiar bonnets sitting on either side of the minister. Suddenly, he remembered the two female Pilgrims who were dressed in similar outfits when they visited Benderloch years earlier. It was then Duncan recognized that these girls were Faith Mission Pilgrims. Afterward, he learned they were Mary Graham from Skye and Jessie Mowat from Aberdeen.

After Duncan was seated, Mary Graham announced her text from Job 33:14: "*God hath spoken once, yea twice, yet man perceiveth it not.*" When she proceeded to preach, Duncan's conscience smarted with conviction. An inner voice was so strong that he had to grip his seat in an attempt to stop trembling. Although he remained at the meeting as long as he could, he continued to shake with fear. Afraid he might make an embarrassing scene in front of his father and those gathered, Duncan left the meeting, picked up his bagpipes and swords, and started out for home.

His departure from the Memorial Hall did not lessen the sense of turmoil that raged in his heart. On several occasions, he fell to his knees at the side of the road and pleaded with God for mercy. Finally, arriving home at two o'clock in the morning, he was surprised to see a light still burning in the crofter's cottage. He slowly opened the door to discover his mother on her knees by the kitchen fire. He was even more moved, and without restraint as he poured out the story of his burdened heart to his darling mother. She listened quietly and then was glad to counsel her son in the simple way of salvation. Because other family members were asleep elsewhere in the cottage, she suggested that he go out alone to the barn and call upon God for salvation. Duncan often told his story:

> *I entered the barn, and falling on my knees among the straw prepared for the horses in the morning, I began to pray. I well remember the prayer I offered. It was in Gaelic!—*

"Lord, I know not what to do. I know not how to come, but if You take me as I am, I'm coming now," and in less time than I can take to tell it, I was gloriously saved kneeling in the straw. I rose from my knees clinging to a simple word of promise: "He that heareth my word, and believeth on him that sent me, hath everlasting life, and shall not come into condemnation; but is passed from death unto life." *I was saved by God's eternal salvation.*

Duncan's early association with the Faith Mission was an avenue that would eventually introduce him to Mr. John George Govan, the founder of the Faith Mission and the man who would make a great impact on Duncan's future life and ministry. That impact and the blessings that followed took Duncan Campbell to Canada, a land to which he felt so indebted.

John George Govan and the Faith Mission would also reach Canada.

CHAPTER 2

How It All Began

Cradled between the towering peaks of Alberta's majestic Rockies are numerous beautiful lakes that give rise to fast-flowing rivers that spread all over the Dominion to make their way north to the Artic, east to Hudson Bay and south to eventually reach the warmer climes of the Gulf of Mexico. Although these mighty waterways begin with small streams, they soon gather momentum to cascade down the mountains, coursing their way through the valleys and across the plains of the vast continent, irrigating fields and prairies as they go.

This Canadian phenomenon bears a striking parallel to the one-hundred-and-thirty-year history of the Faith Mission in Scotland. What began with a flood of blessing in one man's personal experience gave rise to a movement that also gathered momentum to bless and influence many generations of people, coursing its way across frontiers to bring refreshing and blessing to multitudes.

It all began back in Scotland when two Americans returned to Glasgow for another evangelistic mission in 1882. The combined ministry of Dwight L. Moody and Ira Sankey had already made a significant impact on the masses all over the British Isles. They had been so singularly blessed in Glasgow that Christian leaders in the city constrained the two evangelists to return for an extended evangelistic

23

thrust. Moody and Sankey agreed to the invitation, and for six months their passionate preaching and singing fanned the flames of revival all over Glasgow and beyond.

Among those Christian leaders closely associated with the Moody/Sankey mission was Mr. William Govan, a Glasgow City Councillor and what was known in Scotland as a "Bailie," a civic officer and district magistrate. Like his enterprising father before him, William Govan was a prominent and successful businessman in the cotton trade who was held in very high esteem in the city. This great respect was not only due to his valuable contribution to public life and commercial initiatives but also because he was looked upon as a God-fearing gentleman who strenuously opposed the all-too-common social evils of drinking, gambling, and various injustices. Because of his Christian zeal, William Govan was often invited to preach at meetings of different denominations and mission halls.

Behind this public image in business and church, William Govan's greatest contribution and influence to Christian work were in his own family. William's wife, Margaret, the youngest daughter of a Congregational minister, gave birth to their thirteen children, six boys and seven girls, one of whom died in infancy. Right from the beginning of their marriage, William and Margaret conducted family devotions every day. As the family increased and the children grew, they daily prayed with their children and gave them systematic instruction in the Scriptures. This godly and priceless heritage led to five of the six Govan sons becoming preachers of the Gospel and the six daughters also faithfully following their Saviour.

John George Govan was the fourth son and tenth child born into the Govan family, on January 19, 1862. Although among the youngest in his family, he was looked on as the favourite brother, the "blue-eyed boy," by his siblings who endearingly nicknamed him "Donnie." Despite whatever outward charisma he might have exhibited, Donnie never denied his own depravity or the fact that he was a sinner.

Undoubtedly, it was as a result of the godly influences around him and in answer to his parents' prayers that John George trusted the Lord Jesus as Saviour when he was only twelve years old. It happened on the last Sunday evening of the family's annual vacation on the Isle of Arran. Plans were made for the open-air Gospel rally to be held on the rocks at Corrie, overlooking the sea. However, because of the wet weather that evening it had to be convened indoors.

Among those who were invited to speak at the meeting was John George's father, William Govan. Drawing attention to that gathering being the final meeting of the summer, he challenged his listeners, "Will those who have met with us this summer ever be gathered together again?" He went on to point out that the only sure place for them to meet again would be in Heaven, and this was only for those whose hearts were right with God and prepared for eternity.

That Gospel challenge brought deep conviction to young John George Govan. He slipped away to their vacation home, and on the upper floor, under a skylight window, the twelve-year-old boy knelt down. Echoes of thunder pealed over the surrounding hills with the gathering storm, but it was there that John George found peace and forgiveness when he called upon God for mercy. He received new life, eternal life, through Jesus Christ his Lord.

Although his conversion experience was real and set an early course for his future life, John George seldom spoke about the Saviour or showed signs of any spiritual growth during his teenage years. Nevertheless, he was a regular churchgoer and never lost the assurance that he was a Christian and was on the road to Heaven.

At school he excelled at various sports; skating on the frozen lochs in the winter and yachting over the waves on the same lochs in the summer. He also enjoyed essay writing and public speaking. He wrote:

I began to keep a diary when I first entered business at the age of nineteen. I notice that it was chiefly taken up with references to games, business affairs, and political interests. I was a Sunday school teacher and a monitor at the boys' meeting, but it was more a matter of duty than of interest, and the chief talk among the monitors used to be the football match the day before. During the summer we were away a good deal, and I took little to do with Christian work. Any earnestness I showed was fluctuating, and my mind was very worldly. This was my condition before the Lord began to wake me up.

When D.L. Moody and Ira Sankey returned to Glasgow for their six-month evangelistic mission in 1882, John George was in his early twenties and already well established in his own commercial enterprise. His father and brother's involvement in the Moody crusade attracted John George to these meetings. He wrote of them:

D.L. Moody was distinctly and mightily baptized with the Holy Spirit in answer to the prayers of two old ladies, and he came to Glasgow in the mighty power of God. My father was closely associated with them in the work in Glasgow, and I attended about forty of those meetings. They greatly stirred me, and for the first time I began to speak to people about their souls, and feel my need of spiritual blessing.

Moody's passionate preaching and soul-winning zeal greatly stirred and enthused young Govan. At the same time, a battle constantly raged within his heart; although he was a Christian, he was very dissatisfied with the inconsistencies of his up-and-down spiritual experience and longed for a holy and victorious Christian life instead of the mediocrity that constantly dogged and defeated him.

The Salvation Army arrived in Glasgow soon after the conclusion of Moody and Sankey's visit and one of the officers stayed with John George's brother, in the house next door to their family home.

Chapter 2—How It All Began

General Booth and his gifted but frail wife, Catherine, visited the Govan home at "Southpark." That visit brought incalculable blessings to the Govan family through General Booth's powerful preaching and the Salvationists' enthusiastic singing and burning desire for holiness. Similar times of blessing as those enjoyed during the Moody/Sankey mission continued to be outpoured, and hundreds of people were converted, including John George Govan's older brother James.

The combined impact of Moody and Sankey's mission, plus the influences of General and Mrs. Booth and Salvation Army officers, added to his parents' godly example at home, began to shape John George's life. God, the Divine Potter, was moulding this young businessman to be a vessel unto honour. Years later he wrote:

Why God ever chose one so spiritually unfitted for such service, one wonders. But He hath put this treasure in earthen vessels that the excellency of the power may be of God and not of us.

It was a big blow for the Govan family when their father, William, died very suddenly in September, 1883, not long after the end of Moody's mission. Ironically, earlier that night William Govan had preached at a meeting on Hebrews 9:27: *"It is appointed unto man once to die, but after this the judgment."*

The family was called to the father's bedside. Before he died, William Govan singled out his son John George and called him near. With his dying breath, he whispered into his much-loved son's ear, "You are to be a witness for Jesus Christ." Those were William Govan's last words.

Chapter 3

Crisis and Constraint

The commitment and enthusiasm of new converts, prompted by their overflowing love for their Saviour, often outshine that of older Christians who have become stagnant in their spiritual growth. That certainly was the case following the conversion of James Govan, who was known as "Jamie" by his family. Immediately after his conversion to Jesus Christ, he eagerly set about seeking to win others for the Saviour. Jamie's enthusiasm for the Kingdom of God was a rebuke and at times an embarrassment to his younger brother, John George. He spoke of his Jamie's conversion:

> *He had a joyful religion that I did not understand. In the morning I could hear him singing in his bedroom, and I considered this absurd. I did not like people saying "Hallelujah" and tried to avoid coming into too close contact with such persons. I did not mind earthly happiness but religious happiness I did not approve of.*

Jamie not only keenly served the Lord, but he also showed plenty of initiative when he opened a mission hall in Pollokshaws, which he aptly named the "Salvation Hall." He thought nothing of walking five miles to and from the hall in his endeavour to win the lost for Christ.

On the first night that John George accompanied his brother to the Salvation Hall, James asked him to pray. John George was frightened to pray in public, especially in such a large meeting where many people were anxious to seek God. At the end of the meeting, James invited John George to speak and pray with several individuals who wanted to trust Christ as Saviour.

James's keen desire for holiness and service for Christ profoundly challenged John George. He knew that James had already experienced what he called "full salvation," and he longed for a similar encounter with God. He tried to rededicate his life to the Lord and live a little better but was disappointed that his transient closeness to God did not seem to last very long.

After listening to some friends speak of their "clean heart" experience at the Keswick Convention in England, John George became more hungry and thirsty for God and holiness. Whether it was called "full salvation" or "a clean heart," he wanted to know the fullness of God's blessing on his heart and life. A spiritual crisis happened to him at the end of a meeting at the Salvation Hall in Pollokshaws. Of that crisis experience John George later related the following:

> *I remember at the meeting where it came home to me, and God said, "Here is the blessing for you." But I did not yield. The next day I was miserable. At night I went back to a meeting in the Salvation Hall. I went late and sat far back. Two friends got up and testified that they had got a "clean heart." They had been at the meeting of the previous night, and something said to me, "Now, you might have had the same experience if you had trusted."*
>
> *It came at the end of the meeting when my brother called on me to pray. I felt I had to decide there and then. Either I must refuse to pray, or I must trust the Lord to give me the blessing of a clean heart as I prayed. It happened in almost an*

> *instant...I went down on my knees and prayed, yielding my all to God, and trusting Him to cleanse me there and then. I came out of the meeting and said to my friend, "I have a clean heart; I trusted the Lord, and I know that He has done it for me though I do not feel any different." When I got home that night and went down before the Lord, then I knew the difference. The glory of God flooded my soul, and it has been different ever since.*
>
> *It was a new life from that day. The Bible opened to me. I enjoyed it; I saw holiness in it through and through; verse after verse spoke to my heart. I felt the truth of them, and I felt God had brought me to know something of that truth. Hymns that I had never noticed before had new light on them...I was altogether Christ's, and He was the King of my life. Oh, do not think that the chief blessing of a clean heart is a clean heart; the chief blessing is that it is a heart in which Jesus comes to reign. It is Christ Himself who is the chief blessing...do not be taken up with your clean heart, do not be taken up with the "blessing" you have got; be taken up with the King Himself who has come to reign in that heart that has been cleansed and made ready for Him.*

That transforming experience immediately propelled John George into joyful service for Christ at that Salvation Hall. Over the next few years, he and his brothers became absorbed in various soul-winning activities. Many people were led to faith in Christ and scores of Christians were greatly helped in seeking the fullness of God's blessing on their lives. This Christian outreach not only helped develop John George's preaching skills, but he also learned much about the importance, value, and priority of prayer in the Christian ministry. He and his friends joyfully engaged in prolonged seasons of prayer before every evangelistic event, and it was to these prayer meetings that they attributed the blessings that followed.

Besides their demanding program at the Salvation Hall, the Govan brothers attended the Salvation Army on Thursday nights, conducted Bible classes for young people, and then opened another mission hall on Water Street, in Glasgow's Maryhill district.

Running alongside his busy Christian service, John George's commercial venture continued to prosper and had been earning him good financial returns. However, he became convinced that he should be investing his time and energies in more lasting treasures. The words of the Lord Jesus weighed heavily on him, "*Seek first the Kingdom of God and His righteousness.*" He later said:

> *When one allows the Lord to open the eyes and show the glories of His eternal Kingdom, how contemptible and trifling become the things of the world. I can never thank God enough for showing me how little were earthly gains, honours, and pleasures compared with getting souls saved. In eternity we will prove that to get one soul saved is worth infinitely more than getting any amount of fortunes down on this earth.*

Constrained by the challenge of dedicating his life to Christian service, John George applied to become a missionary with Hudson Taylor's China Inland Mission. He was a little perplexed when the Mission Council concluded that John George's health would not withstand the rigours of the Chinese climate and therefore, he could not be accepted.

Afterward, he spoke with Mrs. Catherine Booth about going to India with the Salvation Army. He did not understand it at the time but was surprised when Mrs. Booth dissuaded him by saying, "God has some other work for you to do."

When God closes doors to His children, it is because He has better and more effectual doors to open for them. Back at the Water Street Mission and the Salvation Hall, the Christians were

CHAPTER 3—CRISIS AND CONSTRAINT

praying that instead of the Lord sending John George to China or India, he would use him in Scotland.

God answered those prayers as John George Govan became increasingly burdened and concerned for lost souls in his native Scotland, especially for those who lived in the numerous villages and remote rural areas.

This deepening burden weighed so heavily on young Govan's heart that it quickly developed into a conviction that God was calling him to the ministry of the Gospel in his homeland. Constrained by the love of Christ, John George stepped out of his lucrative commercial business to fully devote his life to preaching the Gospel work in rural Scotland.

CHAPTER 4

The Faith Mission Begins

The friends at Salvation Hall and Water Street Mission pledged to stand with John George Govan and support him in prayer when he initially stepped out to serve the Lord as an evangelist. They had shared with him in many all-night prayer meetings at Water Street and recalled those occasions as "Hallelujah times." It was undoubtedly because of these prayer partners and the volume of prayer from his friends at the Water Street Mission and the Salvation Hall that the presence and power of God were increasingly evident on Mr. Govan's ministry. Those initial prayer meetings set the future pattern for the vital Prayer Unions of the Faith Mission.

Initially, John George wanted to serve God independently as an itinerant evangelist and for this, he adopted Hudson Taylor's principle of living by faith. However, after several very successful evangelistic missions, he realized that the opportunities for Christian work and Scotland's huge spiritual need were far greater than anything he could do alone.

After much prayer and consultation with some highly respected and valued friends, John George Govan founded "The Faith Mission" in October 1886. His primary objective was the promotion of spiritual life and godliness through effective evangelism in Scotland's rural districts and farther afield as God would lead them. John George's chief aim was to seek first the Kingdom of God in soul winning; to strive for Christians to be truly blessed by the Holy Spirit; and to encourage the Lord's children everywhere to pray and present themselves as living sacrifices for God's service wherever He might lead.

Writing in a booklet for candidates for the Mission, *Pilgrim Life*, Mr. Govan expressed the principal aims of the Faith Mission:

> *The Mission was started in 1886, under the guidance of God, we believe, as an aggressive agency to spread the Gospel, which is "the power of God unto salvation." Soul-winning is the primary work of the Faith Mission, and unless it continues to be a soul-saving agency, it does not deserve to exist. This is the first aim in all our efforts. "He that wins souls is wise." "They that turn many to righteousness shall shine as the stars."*
>
> *A second aim is to get professing Christians really and deeply blessed through the power of the Holy Ghost.*
>
> *A third aim is to get the Lord's children interested in His work everywhere, that they may pray, and give, and present themselves a living sacrifice for His service wherever He leads.*

The title, *The Faith Mission*, not only signified that the Mission's workers were trusting God to supply their temporal needs, but John George stressed that the title revealed their entire dependence upon God for the work that had to be done. Faith should be an individual characteristic of each Pilgrim, trusting their Heavenly Father to fulfill all His promises to them as they seek first the Kingdom of God and His righteousness.

Mr. Govan said:

> *The name Faith Mission reflected the fact that the mission had no committee, no financial backing, no influential supporters, but was simply dependent upon God...Faith Mission*

means we are linked on to God, who can do all things and make us more than conquerors. "Have faith in God." What cannot He do for the soul that is given up to Him and trusts Him? He can take the feeble instrument and make it strong in His power, and that is the power we believe in.

The Mission was to be completely interdenominational and thoroughly evangelical. John George Govan believed that it was a waste of time and energy discriminating on labels and names while the world was perishing. Like the Psalmist, he wanted to be *"a companion of all them that fear the Lord, and of them that keep His precepts."*

Early members of the Mission were sent out in pairs and known as "Pilgrims." This name was adopted from Hebrews 11:13 and 1 Peter 2:11 where people of faith were known as "strangers and pilgrims on the earth." Hence, Faith Mission workers were known as Pilgrims for over a hundred years.

Mr. Govan explained his reasons why the first workers were called Pilgrims:

We want those who will foreswear all the comforts of home, all the ambitions of life and the pleasures of the world to go out as "pilgrims (perhaps under this name) and strangers on the earth," and entirely live for God.

In recent years, although the name *Pilgrim* has been replaced with *worker* and *evangelist*, the attitudes that characterized those first workers is still the guiding principle for Faith Mission workers today.

John George Govan and his friend John Colvin were the first two evangelists of the Faith Mission. While John George was preaching in Whitehaven in England, John Colvin began an evangelistic mission in the village of Moffat near Dumfries in October, 1886. John George joined John Colvin to complete that Gospel mission and God blessed them with conversions nearly every night.

To mark the hundredth anniversary of John George Govan's birth, Duncan Campbell wrote:

> *Seventy or eighty years ago the stream of vital Christianity was running low in Scotland. True, the spirit of McCheyne and Chalmers was still alive, but the glorious revival of the Disruption period had darkened to twilight. Moderation had given place to Modernism. Into this blighted field God sent His servant with the message of full salvation, and soon in village, strath [valley] and glen, the dim light became a "great and glorious light."*

That Gospel light dispelled the darkness of spiritual ignorance and indifference, and these two evangelists embarked on a full itinerary of evangelism. During the ensuing year, the power of God marked the ministry of these two men in various villages with many outstanding conversions. This resulted in requests for them to conduct other evangelistic missions or to return to the villages they had already visited. Added to their zeal, sacrificial living, and sincere devotion to God in prayer, they challenged others to join them in the work. By the end of the first year, nine young workers were serving God with the Faith Mission, each depending on God to supply his or her needs and for the anointing of God on his or her ministry.

Year after year the number of Pilgrims increased. At the turn of the century, there were sixty-six Pilgrims who in that same year had conducted one hundred and nine missions in Scotland and Ireland. These itinerant evangelists travelled far and wide, from the Highlands and Lowlands of Scotland, across the Irish Sea, accepting whatever accommodation was provided for them, praying through for blessing, visiting, preaching the Gospel, exalting the Saviour and seeking to stir up the Christians and bring revival to God's people.

The Lord honoured their diligent and sacrificial labours. He answered their prayers: lives were transformed, homes were

Chapter 4—The Faith Mission Begins

united in Christ and whole communities and villages experienced spiritual revival.

While they were grateful for the triumphs of the Gospel, John George Govan and his colleagues were still on the stretch for more blessing amongst God's people, more souls for Christ and more glory to the Lamb of God.

One of the early Pilgrims wrote this of "the Chief," as his Faith Mission colleagues affectionately referred to Mr. Govan:

> *Mr. Govan had great natural gifts, and great grace was upon him. I can recall when he read a passage slowly, thoughtfully—almost hesitatingly, and then he would begin to speak slowly with the Book open. As he kindled to his subject, he would close the Book, and soon the words and ideas of his address would come like a rushing torrent of eloquence which carried all before it and bowed the hearts and heads of his audience like corn before the wind. Like Apollos, "He was an eloquent man, and mighty in the Scriptures."*
>
> *And what power and scorn he had for all that was false and hypocritical, and what dramatic power of description! In one address I will never forget. I think the text was, "Behold the Man!" After a moving description of Christ's sufferings—Gethsemane, the sleepless night, the mock trials, the scourging, the purple robe in mockery, the crown of thorns, the tired face smeared with blood, and the spitting of the cruel Roman soldiers—he paused for quite a while and then said quietly, "My Master!"*
>
> *If I had not crowned Him King and Lord of my life before, I would have certainly done it then. How anyone who was present could have refrained from doing so, I do not know. "My Master!"—that was the secret of his life.*

John George Govan truly was a man highly respected by his colleagues and mightily used by God.

CHAPTER 5

Gospel Growth in Scotland

At the end of the nineteenth century in Scotland, outside of the ranks of the Salvation Army, female preachers were unheard of. Nevertheless, John George Govan believed Joel's Bible prophecy, which foretold: *"Your sons and your daughters shall prophesy"* (Joel 2:28). Accordingly, young female Pilgrims soon became engaged in rural evangelistic work and with great effect. This development was not universally welcomed in rural Scotland. However, John George and his colleagues discounted any discouragement from public opinion and reasoned, "Did not Mary Slessor go from Scotland to Africa to successfully serve God? Therefore, why not welcome dedicated sisters who are prepared to serve God in Scotland?"

The first two female Pilgrims, Agnes Jack and Annie Martin, were volunteers from the original two Prayer Unions at Pollokshaws and Water Street Missions in Glasgow. God's hand was greatly with them, and they made an immediate impact in the village of Drymen, near Loch Lomond, where they conducted their first evangelistic mission. The meetings got off to a slow start as local people adjusted to the novelty of listening to two sisters preach. Undeterred by subtle comments or criticism, the two ladies kept at their task, and within a few weeks, more than thirty people were converted. The first convert at that mission was a local gamekeeper, Mr. John McLean. They did not know it then, nor indeed did Mr. McLean, but in the future, God had a special role for this man in bringing about the Faith Mission Easter Convention to Bangor, Northern Ireland, in 1916.

Throughout the first twenty years of the Faith Mission, the number of dedicated Pilgrims was greatly multiplied. More importantly, like a spreading flame on dry heather, a spiritual revival swept throughout Scotland reaching to the Outer Hebrides, England, Wales, and Ireland. The growth of the Mission and its work was not without opposition and problems. But at that time, many Christians in Scotland considered that the outpouring of the Holy Spirit through the Mission was the greatest spiritual awakening in the land since the famous 1859 Revival. Thousands of people, mostly in rural areas, were converted, numerous Prayer Unions were established, and these were undoubtedly both the cause and effect of those years of blessing.

Arising from this spiritual outpouring, many believers, most of them members of the Prayer Unions, came together for spiritual convocations. In June 1888, the Mission organized the first Holiness Convention in Dunfermline on the Firth of Forth. Prayer Union members travelled from all over Scotland on specially hired trains to hear Mr. Govan and others preach to the assembled congregation.

Another Holiness Convention was also established in the central town of Perth, where again crowds of Christians flocked from all over the country to be spiritually refreshed and blessed through the preaching of God's servants.

The biggest and most notable of these conventions was held in the Victoria Hall at the fashionable seaside resort of Rothesay, the principal town on the Isle of Bute, which was often referred to as "the Gate of the Highlands." God visited the beautiful island with great times of blessing through the Pilgrims' ministry so that many people spoke warmly of the "Rothesay Revival."

It all began in October 1888 when two Pilgrims, Annie Martin (who six years later married John George Govan) and Miss Mitchell, arrived on the Isle of Bute for an evangelistic mission. Small numbers attended the meetings during the first week; fifty people at the most. Notwithstanding these small beginnings, God was with His servants and they steadfastly continued to preach the Gospel night after night. The Holy Spirit began to move on the people. Miss Martin wrote to her friends at the Prayer Union:

Hallelujah! Last night we had a glorious meeting. The hall was crammed with four hundred people, and five souls professed. The Lord was present in power, and many went away deeply convicted, some with tears running down their cheeks. Keep believing! We are having splendid open-airs, and last night we had a proper march along the main streets with a great crowd following us.

For several weeks, the two ladies were constant in their work. They visited, prayed, marched, sang, and preached the Gospel. The prayer meetings continued for hours. The local people realized that something was happening. This was more than another mission; a Heaven-sent revival had come to Rothesay. People came from all over the island to hear the Word of God. Larger premises were needed to accommodate the increasing numbers attending. On weeknights, the girls preached to eight hundred people and on Sunday evenings to fifteen hundred people.

These meetings continued to be well attended for three months, and people were converted nearly every night. Mr. Govan and nine other pilgrims came to preach alongside the original two female Pilgrims, and still the blessings flowed. When John George Govan arrived, he confessed that he was physically weary after a strenuous preaching program. Nevertheless, such was the sense of God's presence and blessing that he felt invigorated in spirit. He wrote of the Holy Spirit's moving on his heart, "He came near and revealed the Name of love. I felt I had so little of that love and was quite broken at His feet."

The influence of the Rothesay Revival on the whole community was such that the local chief magistrate attributed to the work of the Faith Mission the significant reduction in the town's crime rate. More importantly, hundreds of people professed conversion in those meetings, and as a further result of those months of blessing, eight workers joined the ranks of the Faith Mission.

When the Rothesay mission finally closed, two hundred and sixty people came together to form the Rothesay Prayer Union. By this time the Faith Mission was well organized with a proper and much-needed administration. Added to this, a combination of the outpouring of the Holy Spirit in such blessing on the mission and the stunning beauty of the Isle of Bute encouraged the leaders of the Mission to establish its first headquarters at Mount Clare, a large and imposing property in Rothesay. It was at Mount Clare also that the Mission instituted its first Training Home for new candidates. Furthermore, the local Prayer Union became the backbone of the popular Rothesay Convention, which became an annual event.

For many, the Rothesay Convention was the highlight of the year, surpassing those at Perth and Dunfermline. People, young and old, travelled from all over Scotland and beyond to hear God's servants preach the Word of God and to have their souls blessed, refreshed, and challenged. Mr. Govan poured out his soul as he joined other servants of God to minister the Word of God while Mrs. Govan rendered solos most evenings.

Rev. Andrew Murray, the noted author and Keswick speaker from South Africa and good friend of Mr. Govan, was amongst those who spoke at the Rothesay Convention in 1895. In 1898 he sent his personal greetings to the Convention:

> *Will you please give my greetings to the beloved members of the family of God who gather at your Convention this year. As my prayer for you I send the text—may all be able to say it when they part—*"We beheld His glory, the glory of the Only-begotten of the Father, full of grace and truth. And of His fullness have we all received, grace for grace." *May our Father, by His Holy Spirit, give all the vision of the "glory" and experience of the "fullness."*

Many considered the time spent at the Convention as "Heaven on earth."

Conferences, such as that at Rothesay, demanded a lot of planning and preparation. Mission workers were drawn from all over the country to help prepare the venue. During the week of the Convention, each worker had his or her stewarding duties.

At the turn of the century, the Faith Mission evangelists were already working in Ireland, and numerous Prayer Unions had been established across the island. John George Govan was invited to preach at the International Police Association in Belfast in 1891. Subsequently, contacts were made in numerous rural areas throughout Ireland and Prayer Unions were formed. From these areas, dozens of young volunteers became Faith Mission Pilgrims.

It is true to say that great doors often swing on small hinges. When John George Govan arrived in Ireland for the first time in May 1891, he did not know how important or far-reaching that visit would be. While he attended the International Christian Police Association Conference, he was introduced to three sisters, May, Emma, and Helena Garrett.

The Garrett sisters were struck by this young man's zeal for God and the power of God on his ministry and subsequently invited him to send Pilgrims to conduct an evangelistic event at their home in Blackrock, County Dublin. Horace Govan and Pilgrim Corsie travelled to Ireland expecting to stay in Blackrock for less than a week. God so blessed the meetings that they continued for four weeks.

In 1916 the Garrett sisters sold their home in Ireland and journeyed to South Africa on the last passenger boat to sail to that continent during the Great War. It was their intention only to stay in Africa for a year. Shortly after their arrival, they got involved with the International Christian Police Association, which they considered to be the ministry closest to their hearts.

They soon became intently aware of the great spiritual need in the rural areas of South Africa. With this in mind, they wrote to John George Govan requesting that the Faith Mission send Pilgrims to Africa. Mr. Govan turned the challenge to the sisters and encouraged them to start the work themselves. The three ladies did not shrink from answering that challenge. Together with Miss Cameron, a former Pilgrim, they devoted their time, means, and energies spreading the Gospel message in rural South Africa.

As the years went by, they gave themselves to much prayer and waiting upon God about the future of their work. The outcome of this was the formation of the Africa Evangelistic Band in 1924.

CHAPTER 6

Departures and Arrivals

1927 was a pivotal year for the Faith Mission. The famous Ulster evangelist, William Patterson Nicholson, preached with great power to packed churches at the annual Faith Mission Easter Convention in Bangor, Northern Ireland that year. Also at that time, more than a hundred Faith Mission workers were enthusiastically engaged in multiple missions all over the British Isles and in South Africa.

Also in 1927, John George Govan, the Chief, was the principal speaker at the Faith Mission's Convention at Perth in Scotland. It was to be his last Faith Mission Conference. During that Perth Convention, John George Govan went to be with the Lord. It was ironic if not providential that his final address was with great intensity and fervour as he preached about Elijah and Elisha travelling to the Jordan together before Elijah's translation to Heaven. That night he suffered a stroke, and after three days of unconsciousness, he passed into the presence of his Lord. He had energetically run his race, bravely fought his fight, and faithfully finished his course, leaving behind a legacy of blessing for generations to come.

It was a poignant coincidence that on the very day that the earthly remains of the beloved founder of the Faith Mission were being laid to rest in Edinburgh, two Pilgrims, Helen Gibb and

Phoebe Rowdon, were sailing from Liverpool on their way to Canada. These two young women were on their way as ambassadors for Christ to pioneer the work of the Faith Mission in the great Dominion. They had volunteered in answer to an appeal from Mr. Govan earlier that year for those who were willing to trust God and serve the Lord far from home.

At the end of January 1927, the Mission's Chief received a letter from the Rev. W.A. Nisbet, minister of St. John's Presbyterian Church in Toronto, with an appeal for the mission to consider opening a branch of the Faith Mission in the Dominion. Here is a copy of that letter:

JAN. 17TH, 1927

Dear Mr. Govan,

I have been thinking a great deal of you all of late and of the great work of the Faith Mission. There is tremendous need here for something of a similar character. The Alliance is doing a splendid work but along different lines. I am afraid there is great ignorance of the Way of Life both in our cities and country folks. I have been wondering if anything could be done in the way of having a Faith Mission Centre here.

Last week at our missionary meeting, discussion arose about undertaking some definite spiritual home mission work and I took the opportunity of telling them of the Faith Mission, which greatly interested them. They requested me to find out, if I could, something of the origin of your work and whether or not there was any possibility of you extending it to Toronto.

I cannot say what financial assistance they would be prepared to give, but I believe they would give heartily if they knew the nature of the work. We have a fairly strong middle-class congregation here with 1,100 members or a little more. The past year has witnessed many changes in going and coming. The secular and worldly side has almost disappeared

Chapter 6—Departures and Arrivals

from our work and with it many who could not see eye to eye with us. But our increase far exceeds our loss, and they have come from all denominations, Anglican, Methodist, and Plymouth Brethren, of the open type. There are still a few who hold office and give no evidence of conversion. I feel they will make a big effort at our annual meeting (on Wed. 26th Jan.) to restore at least the annual Congregational concert and social which was also of a secular nature till last year. How things will go, one cannot say but the promises have been all assuring us of victory of a real purging. My hope, and the hope and prayer of many, is that every secular thing may soon be swept out, and the great awakening come...We have only to stand still and see the salvation of the Lord. Praise His name! We have some of the Faith Mission converts here.

I do long to see the day when there will be a band of young people here and the whole surrounding district of the type of workers you turn out from your Training Home who will publish the glad tidings in this entire district.

I hope you will forgive me for encroaching on your precious time. I had several times thought of writing you but I felt I was only a solitary individual; however when our missionary executive of their own accord asked me to do so, I felt that the hand of God was in it.

With my kindest regards to Mrs. and Miss Govan and other F.M. Friends.

I am,
Yours in our Coming Lord,
William A. Nisbet

William Nisbet, who originally left Ireland for the Presbyterian ministry in Canada, had clear memories of the Faith Mission workers in his homeland and longed to see their ministry introduced to Canada. His appeal prompted Mr. Govan to circulate a letter among all Faith Mission workers to see if there was someone who could answer this "Macedonian call" from Canada.

During the summer of 1927, three pilgrims, Helen Gibb, Phoebe Rowdon, and Agnes Waugh, were conducting a Gospel campaign in Southend-on-Sea on England's east coast when Mr. Govan's letter arrived. In their daily prayer times for the Mission's work and workers, they directed their prayers to "the Lord of the harvest" to "send forth labourers" to Canada.

While they engaged in corporate prayer about the matter, the Lord spoke to them. Although God had been blessing their evangelistic work, they had entered the Faith Mission on the same basis as all the other volunteers—ready for anything that God might indicate. They never imagined that God would want them to answer this call to Canada. However, the word came clearly from Mark 6:32, *"And they departed...by ship privately."*

Being assured that God was leading them to take this step, the three ladies replied to Mr. Govan's appeal, indicating how God had guided them. In due course, the Mission Council accepted all three ladies for this venture. Helen Gibb and Phoebe Rowdon were designated to go as soon as possible, and Agnes Waugh was to follow afterward.

As the ship, the *SS Letitia,* slowly pulled out from its moorings on Liverpool's River Mersey, Helen and Phoebe were glad that Mr. Govan, who was now at home with the Lord, had got a glimpse of the Faith Mission's future work in Canada. These two pioneers were not only ambassadors for Christ, but they were also ambassadors for the Faith Mission.

John George Govan's passion for the lost was something he endeavoured to impart to his colleagues in the Faith Mission. Speaking to them he said:

> *Grace, grit and gumption are needed by Pilgrims. God has taken men and women from behind the plough, behind the*

> counter, from crofts and fishing boats, and made them mighty in prayer and in preaching the everlasting Gospel. Academic qualifications are not to be despised, but the one indispensable qualification for soul winning is the baptism of the Holy Ghost. We have no power of our own, but living faith links us to His power. If all of us...were baptized with the Holy Ghost and with fire, what an awakening and conflagration there would be! Surely such an experience is worth waiting for and sacrificing all for.
>
> Unless we are in living touch with the Lord, we will not be equal to the task. I consider the "morning watch" one of the most important things in the life of a Faith Mission worker. Out of touch with Christ, we become powerless, formal, and a burden in our work...Time needs to be set apart for special seasons of waiting upon God for spiritual renewal if we are going to be "more than conquerors." We need to know experimentally the "renewing of the Holy Ghost."

The Faith Mission was his legacy, and these two Pilgrims were taking it to Canada. Even then they were not aware that the impact of the Mission had already touched Canada before they had arrived.

In 1901 two Faith Mission evangelists had a remarkable mission in Tarbert, a village on Loch Fyne, Scotland. A report of that mission appeared in *Bright Words*:

> For the first few weeks, it seemed as if the devil was going to have the victory, as there was so much coldness in many of us, God's children, and a fearful indifference in the unsaved. In the third week of the mission, the Lord brought us to wait on Him in earnest believing prayer for an outpouring of the Holy Spirit. In the fourth week, the Lord gave us the joy of seeing the first convert taking his stand for Jesus, and since then He has been continually adding souls to our number.

> *This has been a special time of refreshing from the presence of Lord. There have been many years since such evidence of the work and power of the Spirit of God, or a mission held for such a length of time that has been so largely attended. The interest never flagged. During the eleven weeks, God has revived the hearts of His own children in a special way...and a great number of unsaved have been brought into saving and living touch with Jesus.*

The fruits of that mission travelled far. Almost thirty years later, two Pilgrims were invited by the United Church of Canada to hold a week of meetings in a large church sixteen miles from Toronto. During those meetings, the minister, a Scottish immigrant, told the people that he had been converted through the two Pilgrims who had conducted an eleven-week mission in Tarbert, Scotland thirty years earlier. He also said that he knew of eight converts from that mission who were now in Christian ministry.

CHAPTER 7

Welcome to Canada

After a rough crossing of the North Atlantic on the SS *Letitia*, Helen and Phoebe were glad to disembark in Montreal at the beginning of the Canadian winter in October 1927. From Montreal, they travelled by train to Toronto where the Rev. William Nisbet and Miss Wilson, a deaconess from St. John's Presbyterian Church, were there to welcome them to Canada. William Nisbet was a little perplexed for he had expected that the Faith Mission Council in Edinburgh might send a contingent of their most stalwart young men. He was, therefore, taken aback when "a bantam brigade" of two diminutive young ladies stepped off the train. He greeted them with, "You poor wee things—you'll get lost in the snow."

Although the girls found the Toronto climate considerably colder than what they had left in Britain, there was a warm welcome and reception for them at Rev. Nisbet's church. Their warm-hearted hosts, Mr. and Mrs. James McArthur, quickly became virtual adoptive parents to Helen and Phoebe.

The newly arrived workers were very encouraged when more than five hundred interested friends gathered at St. John's Church to welcome the Faith Mission to Canada. That first official Faith Mission meeting was indicative of what the Lord had in store for these two girls. Their long dresses and Faith Mission bonnets made

53

them very distinctive, but they quickly gained the label of the two "mighty atoms" because of their infectious enthusiasm for the Gospel, vision for souls, and diligence in their work.

Their first evangelistic mission was held at the United Church in Toronto's Victoria Square in November 1927. During their four weeks of Gospel mission, more than thirty people trusted Christ as Saviour. That campaign was quickly followed by a series of other evangelistic missions in the neighbouring townships of Carville, Markham, Thornhill, Maple, and in the cities of Toronto, Hamilton, and Havelock.

In the spring of 1928, they conducted open-air rallies for children and adults on Wasaga Beach, the longest freshwater beach in the world. At all of these meetings, dozens of people were converted, lives were transformed, homes were greatly blessed, and several of these converts went on into Christian ministry.

Myrtle Wellman, a convert from the mission at Victoria Square United Church, wrote about those meetings afterward:

In November, 1927, Miss Gibb and Miss Rowdon, two Pilgrims of the Faith Mission from Great Britain, came to our church at Victoria Square, Ontario, to hold their first mission in Canada. They held evangelistic meetings for four weeks when about thirty people responded to the invitation to accept Christ as their Saviour.

When the meetings ended my father, Mr. Egbert Avison, was asked to take charge of the Faith Mission Prayer Union which was held at Victoria Square United Church and which continued for several years.

I thank God for sending these two young ladies to Canada to bring the Gospel message of Jesus Christ. I was twelve years old at the time, and as I was attending the meetings often with my family and heard that Jesus died for my sins, I began to realize how much I needed to ask Christ to come into my heart.

Chapter 7—Welcome to Canada

> *I kept putting it off, fearful of going forward when the invitation was given. I remember the days following—oh how happy I was. Then the battles and trials with Satan began, but God gave me strength. Praise His name!*

As news of the blessings and success that attended the Faith Mission workers spread across Ontario's Christian community, invitations came flooding in to conduct more missions in various places. Helen and Phoebe were overstretched to take advantage of so many openings for the Gospel. They were therefore glad when reinforcements arrived from home. Their former colleague in Southend-on-Sea, Agnes Waugh, arrived from Scotland, accompanied by Agnes Dornan from Ireland.

All four ladies were totally committed in zeal and enthusiasm for the Saviour and precious souls. They readily conducted Gospel missions wherever God opened a door. They bravely faced the tough Canadian winters, visiting local farms on foot to share the Gospel with many. On some occasions, they warmed their feet by putting them into the ovens of their hosts' kitchens. Their weekly schedule was taken up with visitation to homes, days and nights of prayer, evening Gospel meetings, open-air meetings and children's meetings during the summer.

A report from a local Burlington newspaper in 1928 told of a mission in Calvary Baptist Church:

> *Quietly, but with great power, has the Spirit of God worked through the meetings held by the Pilgrims of the Faith Mission. Scenes such as we have read about in Ireland and Scotland in recent years have been witnessed in this church. Individuals, young and old, have found salvation in Jesus Christ. Whole families have experienced this wonderful change. At some of the services, the platform has been crowded with kneeling Christians yielding their lives in a*

fuller surrender to the Lord while it seemed the whole church or congregation wept with them. God has visited this church in revival power..."I have never seen such scenes in sixty years of Christian experience," said one deacon.

These Faith Mission ladies followed the same pattern and principles of faith they had employed back in the United Kingdom. Through conferences for spiritual fellowship and Bible teaching, new converts were taught and nurtured in the faith. Part of this discipleship program included setting up Prayer Unions, where the new Christians learned how to pray and support the ongoing work of the Mission in Canada.

After two years of very effective and busy ministry in Ontario, it was evident that the Faith Mission had come to Canada to stay. Rev. Horace Govan, brother of the late John George Govan and recently appointed Director of the Faith Mission in the United Kingdom, visited Toronto with his wife in 1929. During that visit, a Canadian Advisory Council was set up to coordinate and oversee the work. Mr. James McArthur, who opened his home to the first two Pilgrims, became Chairman. The primary business at their initial meeting was to recognize the need for a man to fill the role of District Superintendent for Canada. To this the Faith Mission's leadership in the United Kingdom agreed.

After much prayer had been focused on finding the right person to head up the Canadian work, the Mission approached John Eberstein, who was a Faith Mission Superintendent in the South of Ireland at that time. John Eberstein was converted while a student at the famous Cambridge University in England. At the renowned Keswick Convention, he met John George Govan and was attracted by the passion and commitment he saw in the Faith Mission and its founder. As a result, John Eberstein enrolled at the Faith Mission Training Home in Edinburgh in 1922 to prepare for Christian ministry.

Chapter 7—Welcome to Canada

After working in the Clogher Valley, Northern Ireland, where he led hundreds of people to faith in Christ, he was invited to be the Mission's Superintendent in the South of Ireland. Following three years in that position, an invitation was extended to John Eberstein to lead the new work in Canada. Mr. Eberstein wrote of this invitation:

> *In 1929 the Rev. and Mrs. Horace Govan visited the Canadian work, by which time there were five Pilgrims there. Mr. Govan felt, as did the Canadian Advisory Council that there should be a man in charge as Superintendent, and at another Council meeting of the Faith Mission held in Perth, Scotland, in October, I was asked if I would consider going to Canada.*
>
> *At the time I was working in the South of Ireland, having gone there in 1926 to open up the work for the Faith Mission. I was very happy in the superintendence of the work there, but as I prayed and sought for guidance about this new step, clear direction was given to me through Hebrews 11:8: "By faith Abraham, when he was called to go out...obeyed; and he went out, not knowing whither he went." It was God's word to me confirming His call, and I agreed to go, sailing from Belfast on March 8, 1930, arriving in Toronto on St Patrick's Day.*
>
> *In 1928, the Rev. Roland Bingham of Toronto, the Founder and Director of the Sudan Interior Mission [SIM International], was one of the speakers at the Faith Mission Easter Convention at Bangor, Northern Ireland. It was his first contact with the Faith Mission, one result of which was that the SIM home at 860 College Street, Toronto, became the headquarters of the Faith Mission (in Canada), where a room was always kept for the Pilgrims. This accommodation remained open to us even after we moved our office to 73 Adelaide Street. It was, therefore, to College Street I came on arrival in Toronto.*

The St. John's Evangelical Church, as it was then called, was a great help to us. The minister, office bearers and members could always be relied on for their support. My very first meeting, the day after my arrival, was the rejoining of the Prayer Union in Toronto. I have very clear recollections of those early days—of Mr. and Mrs. James McArthur, our "Pilgrim Father and Mother," and of many other friends who supported us loyally.

In 1932 I came home to Britain to be married with the full intention of returning to Canada. Our plans, however, were most clearly overruled, which seemed difficult to understand at the time, but the pattern became clear less than two years later when I was asked to become editor of Bright Words *(The Faith Mission's monthly magazine).*

Rev. Horace Govan, the new President of the Faith Mission, like his brother John George five years earlier, died very suddenly in 1932. Horace Govan was a gracious and scholarly man, and for forty-two years he had been editor of *Bright Words*, the Mission monthly magazine. The Mission Council concluded that John Eberstein was the most qualified person to succeed Rev. Horace Govan as the magazine's editor.

Although he only served for a little more than two years as the Mission's Superintendent in Canada, John Eberstein left his imprint on the work. He was able to see the Canadian work established and laid the early foundations for the Mission's future years. He returned to the United Kingdom to be editor of *Bright Words*, a position he held for thirty-four years.

Mr. Eberstein became Director of the Faith Mission in 1947 and also became Principal of the Faith Mission Training Home and Bible College for eleven years. After retirement from executive responsibilities in 1968, he was appointed President of the Faith Mission.

CHAPTER 8

Abounding in the Work

Although Mr. Eberstein did not return to Canada, the enthusiastic team of Pilgrims maintained their evangelistic activities by conducting missions in churches and mission halls in many townships and rural communities. Prayer Unions were established, and the Mission gained an increasing number of friends and supporters. Furthermore, the sustained work was bearing fruit. Every conversion is a miracle of God's grace and only eternity will reveal where the ripples of Gospel influence will reach. One example of this was evident in the testimony of Rev. Murray Downey, Dean of the Western Canadian Bible Institute in Regina, Saskatchewan:

> *Though reared in a respectable home, attending church and Sunday school regularly, I do not remember hearing anyone talk of being saved till, at the age of seventeen, I met the Faith Mission Pilgrims in Maple, Ontario. Invited to play the piano for the campaign, I found myself so smitten with a conviction of sin that I trembled while trying to play the closing hymn. At last Christ conquered my stubborn will. I was saved and then nurtured in the Prayer Union meetings.*
>
> *The Lord called me to train for His service first at Moody Bible Institute and then at Wheaton College. During the past number of years, I have been teaching the Bible. Realizing*

> *that there are countless communities where there is a religion without reality, profession without possession, it is my passion to train young people for His service and then to send them forth to all the world to preach the Gospel to every creature.*

Phoebe Rowdon, one of the original pilgrims to arrive, married the Rev. William Nisbet, who had initially invited the Faith Mission to Canada. They remained in Toronto where William Nisbet founded and then became the first pastor of the newly formed Calvary Church on Pape Avenue, Toronto.

Calvary Church continued to be closely associated with the Faith Mission for decades to come and continues to be looked on as the home church of the Faith Mission (in Canada). Great men of God who were friends of the Faith Mission in Britain have pastored this church. After William Nisbet, men of God such as Dr. Arthur Lee from Edinburgh and Dr. Gerald Griffiths, who ministered in Edinburgh and taught at the Faith Mission Bible College, were pastors at Calvary Church. Dr. Griffiths' wife, Kitty Ann, was converted through the work of the Faith Mission in Suffolk, England, as were her parents and brother. Kitty Ann's mother was a Faith Mission worker for some time in the United Kingdom.

Scotsman John Alan Wallace, after studying for two years at the Faith Mission's Training Home in Scotland, embarked on his evangelistic ministry in England and Scotland with other Faith Mission Pilgrims. God blessed his ministry, and he felt completely fulfilled in what the Lord had called him to. He was, however, taken aback when the Mission Council asked him to consider succeeding John Eberstein as Canadian General Superintendent. He related the following about that move:

> *One of the true mottoes of the Mission is* "Seek ye first the Kingdom of God and His righteousness, and all these things shall be added onto you" *(Matthew 6:33). The other*

Chapter 8—Abounding in the Work

being, "Have faith in God" (Mark 11:22). Since the inception of the work in Great Britain, this spirit of dedication and trust has characterized the Pilgrims as they have gone forth in the name and for the sake of their Saviour and Lord. In the experience of the workers, when first things have been put first, the Lord has fulfilled His promise, and the other things have been added.

In 1933, I was asked by the British Council to come as superintendent of the young organization in Canada. I agreed and came believing this to be the will of God for my life. A year later my fiancée, Elsie, joined me and we were married in Toronto from the home of our dear friends, Rev. and Mrs. William Nisbet.

A Council had been formed to give guidance in the Mission's affairs. This has continued through the years and men of highest spiritual calibre have given their best to the Lord's work. Mr. James McArthur, the first Chairman of the Council, gave many years of devoted service. He was followed by Mr. William Walker, who was God's gift to the Mission almost since its beginnings. Equally faithful and devoted to the welfare of the Pilgrims has been Mr. Matthew Leith, Vice Chairman. We thank the Lord for these faithful men and other supportive members of our board past and present.

While we were receiving financial help from Britain, it was felt that sooner or later we would have to launch out and become self-sustaining. So, from the outset of our sojourn in Canada, we suggested to the Council that we cease receiving financial help from the home base and trust the Lord for the needs of the Canadian work. Those opening years were difficult with the aftermath of the Great Depression. Consequently, allowances were very small, money was scarce, and there were testing times, but I record to the glory of God

> that we never lacked. We had no debts; although we were not wealthy, we are healthy and we had a task to perform that superseded financial concern for the work. Above all, we have the consciousness of being in God's will. Still, we had to eat and pay our way, and we proved that God is faithful. The Mission is still continuously dependent on the freewill offerings of God's people, and we thank God for all who have stood with us, and stand with us, in this way.
>
> How the Mission's needs have been met through the years is a constant miracle, and evidence of the faithfulness of God who has been true to His promise in Philippians 3:19: "But my God shall supply all your needs according to his riches in glory through Christ Jesus our Lord."

John Wallace established a Bible college at the Faith Mission headquarters in Toronto, although it only lasted for seven years. The most significant impact of John's enduring leadership was that the Mission's work spread west to British Columbia, east to Nova Scotia and even for a short period into the USA.

John and Elsie were always in great demand. Elsie was a gifted musician, and both of them sang beautifully together.

Added to their own ministry, dedicated Pilgrims, male and female, British, South African and Canadians, were fervently serving God in various townships in Ontario, as the following snippets indicate:

> HAVELOCK: *July 5th, 1936: We are praising God for the salvation of a little boy this week. He has been anxious for a long time. Children are precious in God's sight.*
>
> TERRA COTTA UNITED CHURCH: *September 1936: We praise God for the increase in attendance this week. Also, for four adults seeking salvation. This seems to have caused quite a sensation in the village. Some people are even*

Chapter 8—Abounding in the Work

threatening several of these new converts. Pray for these disturbers and that others who are under conviction may come out this incoming week.

PARK ROAD TABERNACLE: *April 3, 1937: Six of the nine children who professed salvation came out at Victoria Park Gospel Church last Sunday. There has been one adult profession of salvation and five Christians for full surrender. Also, seven backsliders were restored. The attendance is on the increase, but not many unsaved are attending. Five young people came back to the Lord last Sunday night."*

EASTONS CORNER: *September 16, 1939: We praise God that He is here in a definite sense with us. Hallelujah! The indifference, which was so distressing at the beginning of the week, is vanishing and interest in the meetings is awakening. We praise God for increased attendance. Pray that the Holy Spirit will smash Satan's strongholds here and souls will be saved.*

With the continued blessing on the Pilgrims' ministry, the Canadian Council decided to follow the pattern of the Faith Mission's founder and establish a training home where young Canadians could prepare for work with the Mission in their own land. That was realized in 1945 after a long wait to acquire the property of God's choice in Toronto.

The training program began with six students. This was a new venture for them and the Mission, and all were very dependent upon the Lord. Besides supplying their material needs, God also provided Spirit-filled men and women to lead and lecture in the classes. William and Barbara Bee led the training home with the help of Jean Dick (later Mrs. Hanan) and Elizabeth Mather. The Faith Mission Training Home in Toronto continued for seven years, during which time God prepared and used many young men and women who went on to serve God with great impact.

John Wallace maintained a very fruitful life and ministry as Director of the Mission in Canada for over forty years. He went to be with the Lord at the grand age of 105 after a very blessed and full life.

CHAPTER 9

Ontario Outreach

In the initial days of the Faith Mission, God gave to its founder, John George Govan, a promise in Hosea 14:5-6: "*I will be as the dew unto Israel: he shall grow as the lily, and cast forth his roots as Lebanon. His branches shall spread....*" At that embryonic stage of the work, the young Scotsman, whose life God had touched, could not have known how much that plant would grow, how far its branches would spread, or how much fruit it would bear for God's everlasting Kingdom.

Those fruitful branches not only spread their reach all over Scotland and its scattered islands, but within a few years, those fruit-bearing boughs extended across the Irish Sea. Devoted Pilgrims zealously preached in churches, mission halls, community rooms, tents and other public venues with a passionate endeavour to lead souls to Jesus Christ. As in Scotland, so also in the Emerald Isle, their labours were not easy and at times were greatly opposed, but God mightily used them in the salvation of the lost, the blessing and sanctifying of His people, and to establish Prayer Unions throughout the island.

Canada is a vast country, thirty times the size of the British Isles. The Mission's work not only took root and became a very productive ministry in the greater Toronto vicinity; soon its stems began to spread to other parts of Ontario and beyond.

Eastern Ontario

Early in the history of the Faith Mission, two Pilgrims travelled over four hundred kilometres east of Toronto to the borders of Quebec to conduct Gospel missions. Their influence prompted the owners of the Gospel Hall in Havelock to invite the Mission to take over the premises for their work. This Gospel Hall with its living accommodation became the headquarters for the Eastern District of the Mission's work under the leadership of Mr. and Mrs. William MacFarlane, who came from South Africa.

From Havelock, the Pilgrims fanned out to industrial towns, small villages, and the rural farmlands to reach people for the Lord Jesus. The annual Havelock Conference became a rallying point for Christians in Eastern Ontario throughout the years of World War II. Mr. and Mrs. J. McNeill succeeded the MacFarlanes in this district, and under their direction, three young people from the Havelock area became students at the Training Home in Toronto before going on to give years of service to the work in Canada.

Hester Dougan (later Rendall) a gifted Pilgrim from Banbridge, Northern Ireland, arrived in Eastern Ontario in 1961. She wrote of her time in that district:

> *This whole area is saturated with historical interest because right here the soldiers and pioneers of an emerging nation fought and won battles of many types—and lost a few.*
>
> *Workers of the Faith Mission (in Canada) came into Eastern Ontario well over thirty years ago, and many are the tales we heard of difficult travelling; hard work—and humorous happenings. More important are the accounts of meetings when God came down, souls were saved, and people changed.*

Chapter 9—Ontario Outreach

Today we find ourselves conducting services in frantic cities, busy towns and more easy-going rural communities. We are deeply grateful to...all our praying friends of the Prayer Unions in Belleville and Oshawa. We all owe them a heavy debt.

Adult, youth and children's work keeps us constantly busy with hundreds of miles being covered every month. Many untouched villages beckon and we plan, in the will of God, to reach these also for the Lord.

Thank God for all His marvellous working in the past, present and we believe, He will do in the future.

On the human side, we have our share of hair-raising adventures; and other amusing situations—we call them "The thrills and spills of Pilgrim life," and they certainly make for a lively involvement!

We are neither heroes nor martyrs, but ordinary people who are privileged to share in taking the message of a full salvation to every age group in Canada.

One afternoon, many years later, my husband answered the phone and a voice asked, "Was your wife named Hester Dougan?"

When the answer was positive, the caller requested, "May I please speak to her?" Imagine my excitement when he gave me his name, and I immediately remembered the place and the meetings.

"Of course I remember you, and you had a sister, too!" At that time we were using the Unit for children's meetings in the afternoon, as well as adult and youth meetings in the evenings.

I reminded the caller that his mother and his aunt also sought and found salvation during those days. They came knocking on the Unit door at 11:00 p.m., saying, "We just have to find peace with God now—we cannot wait until tomorrow." What glorious rejoicing!

> *The caller then questioned, "In all the years since, have you ever wondered what has happened to all those children and youth who were pointed to the Lord?" Excellent and insightful question!*
>
> *What a joy it was to hear this man, his wife and their children, all true believers in the Lord Jesus, are actively involved in their church's activities.*

* * * *

Southwestern Ontario

Under Mr. Wallace's leadership, many early Pilgrims visited and conducted missions in Southwestern Ontario. The picturesque Niagara Peninsula's main products are corn, wheat, and a variety of fruits. The Faith Mission entered the area in obedience to the great Lord of the harvest seeking for a different produce.

The first Pilgrims who went to the region found it to be fertile ground for the Gospel, and they were greatly used to lead many to faith in Christ. Some missions continued for five and six weeks before the workers moved on to another location. Those Pilgrim pioneers laid good groundwork for the Mission, and others who followed later greatly benefitted from their labours.

Horace Wahl was converted in a mission conducted by Mr. Wallace in Stevensville, Ontario. Here is his testimony:

> *I remember when I could not honestly answer the question, "If I died today am I 100% sure of Heaven?" That takes me back to 1959/60. The church I then attended planned special services, and the Faith Mission of Canada was invited. Brother and Sister Wallace came for two weeks and preached the Word.*
>
> *I was born in Germany during the time when Hitler and*

Chapter 9—Ontario Outreach

the Nazi Party were in power. At the age of six I became a member of the Nazi Young People's Movement, marching to the motto, "Today we have Germany, and tomorrow we conquer the world." The philosophy of Hitler had a great effect on my life. In 1945, Easter Sunday, the American allies invaded our city, and for the first time, I realized that Germany had lost the war.

In the years that followed, many people, including myself, flocked back to church to look for some answers and security. So, in 1948, I was confirmed, being told that everything between God and me would be in order, and I could take my First Communion. I believed, if I did not commit any major crime or do anything too bad, that this matter was taken care of for the rest of my life.

The years that followed were filled with the pleasures of this world and a desire to explore the New World. In 1954 I immigrated to Canada and soon fell in love with the country and its people. Through working and living on a farm, I had the opportunity to attend an evangelical church. Soon I recognized that there was more to the Christian life than I had experienced. It was during those special meetings in 1959/60 that I realized for the first time I was a sinner and lost; I was condemned and on my way to Hell; I also learned that Jesus paid my debt on the cross and that I must repent and receive Him as my Lord and Saviour.

I am happy today that I responded to God's love and forgiveness and I am grateful to the Lord for the Faith Mission's ministry and their faithfulness in preaching Christ.

Over the years it has been a pleasure for me to work with the Faith Mission, especially in the Daily Vacation Bible School, and we have seen over and over again God at work through His Son, our wonderful Lord and Saviour.

May God's grace, peace, and blessing continue on the Faith Mission ministry.

Many other testimonies were given of how lives were changed, families blessed and churches greatly stirred.

CHAPTER 10

Passing the Baton

The expansion of the Faith Mission's work on many fronts meant that Mr. Wallace and the Canadian Council needed to look for District Superintendents to guide, grow, and oversee the work.

For that reason, Hugh and Anne Jamieson were invited to lead the work in the Niagara Peninsula region in 1958. Hugh had trusted the Saviour as a teenager at a Faith Mission meeting in Northern Ireland. He immediately gained the assurance that he had passed from spiritual death unto life and soon began to grow in his new-found faith in Christ. During his spiritual development, God challenged and spoke to him at another Faith Mission meeting. He spoke about that in the following way:

July 12, 1946, was another memorable day in my life. I had been to Ballymena Faith Mission Conference, and God spoke to me about full-time Christian service. This was not the first time I heard this challenge. God had been speaking to me about this for several months. About midnight I was standing beside a peat stack when a voice seemed to say, "Hugh, are you willing to go?"

I knew it was God speaking and after a moment I replied, "Yes, Lord." That clear call set my course for the Faith Mission Bible College, which I entered in October, 1947.

Following graduation and while working with the Mission in Scotland, Hugh met Anne, who later became his wife. Hugh and Anne volunteered to join Mr. Wallace's team of Pilgrims who were working in Southwestern Ontario. After they arrived in Canada in 1958, Hugh and Anne gave their energies to the daunting challenge of evangelism with real enthusiasm. In time they purchased a home for the Mission in Hamilton and Hugh became the District Superintendent for Southwestern Ontario region, an area that takes in the Niagara Peninsula.

Anne Jamieson wrote about their early days in the work:

When we arrived in Canada, it was decided that the city of Hamilton was the most suitable centre from which to carry out our work. With the help of Mr. and Mrs. Ed Barton (the latter was an early convert of the first missions in Canada), accommodation was found and contacts made with various evangelicals in the city and surrounding areas.

Our work began with a mission held at Fruitland Chapel, near Hamilton, and the first convert was a young married woman who constantly witnessed wherever she went. She was often seen at one of Hamilton's busy street corners engaged in tract distribution. This young woman was the "first fruit" of many scores, mainly young people and teenagers, who found Christ as their Saviour and crowned Him Lord of their lives.

Soon Hugh was visiting Bible schools, speaking at Bible conferences, conducting Faith Mission rallies and engaging in evangelistic missions. He was constantly on the go, and many people in Ontario still remember his powerful voice, his passion for reaching the lost for Christ and his determination to let no difficulty stop him from doing what he felt God was asking him to do.

Hugh quickly endeared himself to the people. He spent thousands upon thousands of hours visiting from door-to-door, inviting

Chapter 10—Passing the Baton

both young and old to meetings. He preached hundreds of sermons and told numerous children's stories. Hugh had an incredible gift of knowing how to motivate people to become involved in evangelism. Men especially appreciated Hugh's robust style and under his direction, the layman's organization, "Faith Mission Men," multiplied and prospered.

During the summer of 1960, Hugh erected a tent in a field into which boys and girls crammed to sit on the grass and listen to Hugh and Anne tell Bible stories. This was the beginning of their Vacation Bible Schools, which soon multiplied and became a regular feature of their summer work. Countless numbers of boys and girls trusted Jesus Christ as Saviour and many children were enrolled in a Bible study course. This also became an incentive for parents to join their kids in studying the Scriptures.

Hugh organized a young people's retreat at Niagara Christian College in May 1963. It was so successful that he went on to organize an annual "May Youth Weekend." On several occasions, the Holy Spirit moved, resulting in great brokenness and blessing. Hugh followed this up with annual fall and winter retreats for young people.

Following the success of the Vacation Bible Schools and the young people's retreats and rallies, Hugh arranged a thriving Young People's Fellowship. Besides meeting for the special rallies and weekends, YPF groups were formed in various districts. Many who are not so young today can look back to the time and place where Hugh knelt beside them as they surrendered their lives to the Saviour.

The idea of a Mobile Mission Unit was suggested to overcome the difficulty of finding suitable halls in rural districts. The Lord provided the need for such a unit with a seating capacity for forty adults or seventy children plus compact accommodation for two workers. The first Faith Mission Mobile Unit was dedicated in April 1963 and put to good use for years afterward.

A second unit was later purchased and was used by Raymond and Sandra Thompson in evangelism in many communities in Southwestern Ontario. They shared one story from that venture:

In the fall of 1976 we moved to the Chatham area and lived in a small village. Our first set of meetings was in the mobile chapel which we parked beside a local church in the village of Duart. We planted the seed of the Gospel but there was no outward response from the children or youth who attended.

A few years later we received a phone call late one evening. The caller apologized for phoning so late but was compelled by the Holy Spirit to tell us that at a youth event that night some young people gave testimony that they had come to receive Jesus Christ as Saviour as a result of those meetings in the mobile chapel. We rejoiced together on the phone and also rejoiced in the Scripture Isaiah 55:11: "So shall My word be that goeth forth out of My mouth: it shall not return unto Me void, but it shall accomplish that which I please, and it shall prosper in the thing whereto I sent it."

In the mid-1960s a group of laymen on the Niagara Peninsula became concerned about the need for more roadworthy transport in the Hamilton area. A Transportation Committee was set up to provide a suitable vehicle. Further to this, the same Committee made itself available to help the work of the Faith Mission. A letter sent to the members of the Transportation Committee in August 1969 announced,

"Faith Mission Men," a new movement in the Faith Mission that has been pioneered by the Transportation Committee will be officially launched on Tuesday, September 9, 1969, at Jim Campbell's house.

At that meeting, they set out the purpose and plan for the movement: promoting the work of the Mission, organizing rallies

Chapter 10—Passing the Baton

and retreats, and recruiting dedicated Christians to help in the extension of Christ's Kingdom on earth. Their statement was prefaced with these words:

Faith Mission Men is a self-sustaining organization of men within the framework of the Faith Mission and is under the complete supervision of the Faith Mission Council.

These men zealously stood together with the Faith Mission evangelists in missions, rallies, retreats, and maintaining the Mission's properties and vehicles. Their work was greatly appreciated by Hugh Jamieson, who wrote of the contribution these men had made in supporting various Gospel missions:

There are scores of small towns and rural communities in Southwest Ontario that had no evangelistic mission in living memory. Many hours of door-to-door visitation often resulted in five to fifteen adults or thirty to fifty children at the meetings. It is necessary to remember that most of these people would not be exposed to the Gospel if the Faith Mission (in Canada) had not gone there.

For years, Faith Mission Men teams visited every home in Dunnville and organized open-air services at the bandshell every Sunday evening during July and August. They organized specific work bees to do maintenance on Mission properties. Later, after the Campbellville Centre was purchased, the men volunteered to do the bulk of the renovating and upgrading work.

The Mission's indebtedness to these dedicated people cannot be overstated. Many of them are now with the Lord. Unfortunately, the organization no longer functions as it used to. Today, younger men with fresh vision and a heart for God and the lost are needed to take up the mantle for the present generation.

When Dr. Martin Lloyd Jones preached on the story of Elijah and Elisha, he quoted Elisha's question, *"Where is now the Lord God of Elijah?"* and then he ended his sermon by stating, "He is waiting for today's Elishas to take up the mantle."

Hugh and Anne continued in Hamilton until 1980 when he was invited to succeed Mr. Wallace as General Director of the Faith Mission (in Canada). Just as he had been dynamic and energetic as an evangelist, so Hugh continued as Director. It was a very sad day for the Faith Mission (in Canada) when after a long period of battling with illness, God called him home in 1987.

CHAPTER 11

Northlands

Canadian winters can be extremely severe, and each year they blanket the whole country in a covering of deep snow and ice, except for the milder Lower Mainland of the western province of British Columbia. Even south of Canada's Artic region, temperatures can plummet to below -30°C, and these conditions bring many challenges for numerous communities. It also provides excellent opportunities for the population to engage in their national ice-skating sports on frozen lakes and ponds.

Faith Mission workers were also challenged to preach the Gospel *"in season and out of season"* to people who lived in the towns, villages, and isolated farmlands in Northern Ontario. During the fall and winters, a window of opportunity opened for evangelism in Ontario's north. Snow ploughs kept the highways open, but in the early days, cars often seized up in the freezing conditions.

However, spurred on with the Saviour's command to take the Gospel to *"every creature,"* dedicated Pilgrims were prepared to brave the elements to conduct missions in those colder climes. They discovered that even though the weather was cold, the welcomes were warm and the families friendly. Homes, schools, community halls, and churches opened their doors to allow the Pilgrims to conduct Gospel missions. From town to town—

Thornloe, Rouyon, Noranda, Farmborough, Matachewan, and Algonquin Park—only a few of the places various workers presented and preached the Gospel, visiting from home to home and leading many to personal faith in Jesus Christ.

John A. Wallace, the former Director of the Faith Mission (in Canada) who went to be with the Lord in his 105th year, said before he died, "If I had my life to live over again, I think I would be a children's evangelist." His reasons were primarily because when a child is saved, a whole life is saved for the Saviour. Also, children are so impressionable that it is important to reach them before their tender minds become corrupted by the world. Furthermore, often by reaching a child for Christ, it can be an open door that leads a whole family to the Saviour also.

When the Faith Mission work began in the north in 1959, it was mostly in one-roomed schools. The Pilgrims found that the co-operation of the teachers was invaluable. Because the school bus picked children up after school, it was not practical to organize an after-school club. However, the children were willing to give up a half of their lunch break while the teachers allowed another half hour of class time. That meant it was possible for the Pilgrims to hold services for an hour each day for a whole week in various locations.

In some schools, the Pilgrims were permitted to have their meetings during school hours. They were given thirty minutes in each classroom to teach choruses, read the Bible, and give a lesson. This meant that the evangelists spent the whole day going from class to class, teaching the boys and girls about Jesus. It was a priceless opportunity.

When the Pilgrims arrived at one school, they discovered that examinations were in progress. They politely excused themselves and said they would return on another occasion. The teacher would have none of it. She told the class to turn their papers over

Chapter 11—Northlands

as the missionaries had arrived. She then handed the time over to the Pilgrims to teach the Bible.

It was sometimes difficult under these circumstances to have personal dealings with the children, but God always has ways and means. One day a boy spoke to the Pilgrims after they had parked their car and said, "I simply don't understand about being a Christian." After a short conversation with the lad, they had the joy of pointing him to the Lord Jesus. Two other girls thought they were too late to speak to the workers because they were closing the school door. One said, "We really wanted to be Christians, but we are too late." These two girls had learned thirty-one verses of Scripture in a short time, and the Pilgrims were quick to tell them that they were not too late, there was still room and time to accept Christ, and they did.

During a visit to the Prayer Union in Robillard, the Faith Mission workers were thrilled and touched to hear several young people tell how they had decided to accept the Lord as children in the school services. It was even more encouraging to hear them pray for the work and workers of the Faith Mission (in Canada).

Wasaga Beach, a town in Simcoe County, is one hundred and forty-five kilometres north of Toronto. This popular summer resort is situated on the southern end of Georgian Bay and has the longest freshwater beach in the world.

The Faith Mission first entered Wasaga Beach in 1928, soon after the first workers arrived in Canada. This visit developed into an enduring work over the following decades. Mrs. Wallace wrote of that development:

> *The Master spent much time preaching and teaching by the Sea of Galilee, and in spending our summers on the beautiful Georgian Bay, we feel we are, to some extent, following in His steps. Has He not bade us sow beside all waters?*
>
> *The summer work at Wasaga Beach and district presents a great challenge, but is also a wonderful privilege. For six*

> weeks or more, we Pilgrims live in the fresh outdoors, sitting on the beach in the bright sunshine, breathing in the good air that comes across the Georgian Bay. However, pleasant though this may be, it is not our main objective for coming to this part of the country. The boys and girls are here, and we want to reach them for God.
>
> How did the Faith Mission come to work in the Wasaga area? Well, in the early days of the Mission in this land, the Pilgrims came to the Beach primarily for an open-air ministry to adults, and this was carried on for many years. But things change as the years go by, and it is not possible to have open-air services on the Beach, so we concentrate on reaching boys and girls. Their young hearts are receptive to the truth of God's love for them, and many respond and yield their lives to the Saviour.
>
> Through the years, different parts of the Beach area have had meetings. We visit Brock, Woodland, and Allenwood beaches along with Wasaga itself, calling the children by means of a public address system and taking them to the beach by truck.
>
> It is impossible to give an adequate account of the efforts to make Christ known over the years at Wasaga Beach and the surrounding areas. Visiting the cabins and cottages has occupied much of the Pilgrims' time. While enrolling one of the little boys recently, he looked up brightly and said, "My mommy used to come to these meetings when she was a girl." When we asked her name, we remembered her.

Another report in a 1969 issue of *Life Indeed* recorded the following:

> Some children come every year for nine or ten years. On the four beaches where we work, there is an enrolment of 600 children with an aggregate attendance of over 4,000 boys and girls. Some of these children attend every day for seven weeks.

Chapter 11—Northlands

In 1947, friends and Mission workers combined to build a cottage, the Wasaga Cottage, for the Faith Mission workers on Moseley Street in Wasaga. The cottage provided accommodation for the Pilgrims and was also a venue for meetings and hospitality for young people.

A former Faith Mission Board member, Phillip Ali, told of a near-tragic incident that happened at the Wasaga Cottage. A group of friends arrived at the cottage to help renovate the building. Among them was Floyd Krick, who was accompanied by his wheelchair-bound wife, Eileen. One morning during the week, Floyd got Eileen out of bed and ready for the day. Without them knowing, someone had removed the wooden steps from outside the cottage's front door, intending to have them replaced with a new structure. Quite unsuspectingly, Floyd wheeled Eileen and chair through the front door when suddenly, the wheelchair and Eileen suddenly dropped out of Floyd's hands to the ground. Although Floyd was shocked, Eileen just burst out laughing and then looked up at her husband and exclaimed, "Oh, Floyd!" Both of them quickly laughed off the incident, but at the same time, they were grateful to God for His protection and that this fragile lady did not suffer any irreparable hurt.

The Mission's vision to reach children has been clear from its beginning in 1927 and every summer through July and August, a team of workers evangelized on Wasaga Beach and surrounding beaches by conducting meetings for kids and adults. Sadly, a by-law introduced in 1988 prohibited preaching on these beaches. The Mission team, therefore, moved to local parks so that the ministry to kids could continue. Today, many adults trace their conversion to those meetings on the beaches and parks around that lake. A similar ministry was also carried out at the Crescent Beach in British Columbia. It is no exaggeration to say that thousands of children and young people have professed faith in Christ at these meetings.

For several decades teams of Pilgrims also conducted summer beach meetings at Port Dover, a town located on the shores of Lake Erie and one hundred and thirty-five kilometres south of Toronto. Many people also look back to the meetings at Port Dover as the place they found Christ as Saviour. Robert Goldie told of a remarkable testimony of a Lifeguard who trusted Christ:

> *In 1953 we offered to help Miss Gibb during our week's holiday at Port Dover. While there we noticed that the lifeguard at the beach was very helpful in seeing that the children behaved. After the meeting each morning he helped us organize the long rope for the children's Tug-of-War. When that was finished, we all rushed into the water for a swim.*
>
> *After returning home, we received a letter from Miss Gibb telling us that the lifeguard said that on Sunday night he had done it, meaning he had got down on his knees and given his heart to the Lord. At Port Dover, the lifeguard got saved.*

The Faith Mission's Chief, John George Govan, stated early in the Mission's history, "Soul-winning is the primary work of the Faith Mission, and unless it continues to be a soul-saving agency, it does not deserve to exist. This is the first aim in all our efforts. 'He that wins souls is wise.' 'They that turn many to righteousness shall shine as the stars.'"

Chapter 12

British Columbia

Mr. and Mrs. William MacFarlane, who had led the work in Eastern Ontario for several years, left Ontario in March 1939 to open up the Mission's work on the West Coast. It is almost amusing how this transition developed. John McGall of Vancouver, a man saved from a life of drunkenness when Pilgrims visited his hometown in Scotland, sent a donation to the Mission with the following note: "When I read of your Pilgrims wading through snow, I wonder why you don't send workers to B.C. where there is little snow."

John McGall's invitation came as a seal to the MacFarlanes who for health reasons needed a change of climate. The milder climes of B.C. suited this South African couple, and very soon they adapted to the more favourable conditions. Not only did they adapt, but they also became so invigorated that they were able to continue in the Mission's work in Western Canada for almost thirty years.

Other workers soon followed the MacFarlanes to the Pacific Coast, and Scottish immigrant, John McCall, rejoiced when he saw five Pilgrims arrive—in "bonnets," just as he had seen them in Scotland.

Mrs. Jean MacFarlane related some recollections of those early years in British Columbia:

We reached Vancouver and were warmly welcomed by John McGall, who had been waiting for us. Soon we arrived at his cottage, and what a heartwarming time ensued as we spoke of the ways of the Lord. Later, he rose to his feet and said, "Take a look around this cottage. If it suits you, you are welcome." That night, with a roof over our heads and beds on which to rest, we two Pilgrims, greatly marvelling at the way the Lord had led, bowed our heads and worshipped.

Our benefactor wasn't long in getting on the phone to Watson Smillie of Blackbraes, Sam Campbell of Newtownards, and Archie MacLachlan of Loch Fyne, all of whom had been won to the Lord through Pilgrim efforts. They likewise gave us a warm welcome, then followed thanksgiving and fervent prayer from hearts beating with loyalty and surging with expectation, that God would use the Pilgrims in blessing souls in B.C. Sam Campbell was anxious for us to reach out to the needy Main Street area. An empty store was rented, and here we met with a fine group of teenagers. Watson Smillie lived across the Inlet on the North Shore, and it wasn't long before we crossed the inlet to hold a mission there.

Some months before Pearl Harbour, the Japanese Evangelistic Band missionaries were evacuated from Japan. It was then that Mr. and Mrs. William Bee joined the work in Vancouver, did fervent pioneering in the Fraser Valley and the Cariboo. The Pilgrim band was enlarged by them coming into the ranks of the Mission. Jean Dick and other auxiliary workers soon joined them. What a day of rejoicing it was for John McGall when he saw the five Pilgrims on the conference platform.

Our increased numbers highlighted the need for a headquarters centrally located. How wonderfully the Lord has provided for us since we came West in our dear brother's cottage, and in the basement suite in West Vancouver. But we had to say,

Chapter 12—British Columbia

"The place wherein we dwell is too small for us" *(2 Kings 6:1)*. *So a search began for a commodious house and prayer was made for funds. A large frame house in the Kingsway district was for sale, and from many aspects, it was considered suitable, especially as it was within easy access to the Fraser Valley the Lower Mainland. It required extensive decoration, and faithful friends rallied to the help of the Pilgrims. At the Dedication Service, there was rejoicing among many friends that the full price of the house had been met. Two pillars adorned the entrance hall, each bearing a motto of the Faith Mission: "Have faith in God" and "Seek first the Kingdom."*

1305 East 20th Avenue, Vancouver, B.C., was to see the comings and goings of Pilgrims for the next twenty-five years and more. Each week, without fail, the members of the Vancouver Prayer Union came together there.

Vancouver city afforded many opportunities for preaching the Gospel in churches and downtown mission halls. On most Saturday nights the voices of male Pilgrims could be heard among others in the open-air service on skid row. Work undertaken by the sister Pilgrims was that of The Bible Club for the Kingsway neighbourhood, which brought rich results.

The first Faith Mission outreach on Vancouver Island was at Coombes where Jean Dick and I settled ourselves in the back room of the Community Church. Though times were hard in Coombes, Christians were stirred and strengthened, sinners awakened, and children reached for Jesus Christ. Another mission followed in the United Church in Parksville, and arrangements were also completed for a mission at Nanoose Bay in the smallest church on the Island.

It was at Nanoose Bay—at a later date—that Ella Bone and Isabella McColl were watching the huge trees bowing and swaying in the mighty wind. Suddenly, one crashed to the ground. When they went out to view the fallen giant, a neighbour looked at the girls in amazement.

"Say," she exclaimed, "Do you have God looking after you? That huge tree was swaying and leaning over heavily to your trailer. Suddenly, it seemed as if a Mighty Hand reached down and pushed it over in the opposite direction."

From Vancouver, William MacFarlane forged other openings for the Mission as the workers fanned out from there to surrounding townships and rural areas. They were ready for anything. This was demonstrated in another report from Mrs. McFarlane:

One day in Vancouver, a letter, bearing the cancellation stamp of "Armstrong," arrived. It contained a donation for the work, and in the accompanying letter, we read, "I wonder why you don't send your workers up this way. There is always a barn for you to sleep in."

So Mr. MacFarlane and two auxiliary lads found their way to that part of the upper country, to the home of Jabez Kneller. One slept in the barn, as promised, and the other two slept in a recently acquired car. Meetings were started in the country schoolhouse, where a young mother, rejoicing in her firstborn, made a bright decision for the Lord.

How could the three pilgrims, doing it the hard way, have envisaged the stream of blessing that was to come when the Schweb family let God have His way? Those who were brought to Christ in the potato barn will know in some small measure—and all began when a farmer sent a small donation to the Mission.

In the spring of 1967, we Pilgrims visited the Confederation Train in Vancouver. This very special white train, which was to make its journey right across the Dominion of Canada, had come over from Victoria and was ready to receive Vancouver's citizens. Each of the coaches, beginning from prehistoric times, set forth the unfolding of the Canadian story. The scientific achievements and industrial developments were most impressive. The coaches gave a portrayal of the religious life with the reinforced glass cases in which various symbols of religion were displayed. But the BIBLE—"the most valuable thing this world affords," as is stated in the Coronation Ceremony of the British Sovereigns, was not in evidence.

On reaching home, we got in touch with the Canadian Bible Society and Gideons International, as well as ministers of various denominations. Letters were sent to the Minister of the Interior, who later became Secretary of State and, as such, wrote informing us, "A Bible has been put aboard the Confederation train." This was done in a special ceremony before the train reached Edmonton, Alberta.

Pilgrim Cathie Macaulay, who trained with the Mission in Toronto, travelled extensively in B.C. with various colleagues to hold missions for children and adults. Mr. MacFarlane said to her when she embarked on this work, "You are going out, not just to sow the Good Seed, but to stump and cultivate the ground by hard work and prayer."

Cathie did plough, sow, and witnessed a great harvest in her labours for Christ. She was a versatile and very gifted evangelist to children and adults. Her musical skills also enhanced her work. Here are a few snippets from Cathie's travels:

As the early pioneers faced the challenge of clearing and cultivating land before seed could be sown, so the Pilgrims have returned to outlying places year after year, renewing contacts, breaking down barriers, establishing confidence, and sowing seed. As a result of prayer warriors meeting at the Throne of

Grace with us, some seed has sprung up into life and Christian maturity. No doubt some seed has fallen by the wayside, but some are lodged in minds and hearts and will be used by the Holy Spirit, in His time, to help bring conviction, repentance, and saving faith.

As accommodation presented a great problem in many areas, Mr. and Mrs. MacFarlane had a God-given inspiration, which materialized in buying two homemade second-hand trailers. These house trailers were named The Chief, *after Mr. John George Govan, the Mission's founder, and the other* The Pioneer, *after John McGall, the man responsible for praying the Faith Mission out to British Columbia. The Chief was the first trailer to be used in the Okanagan Valley. This valley stretches over 200 kilometres north from the U.S. border and about 500 kilometres from the Pacific Coast.*

In the fall of 1948, Mr. MacFarlane and Keith Wilcox, Marion Swank and I headed for the Interior. At Six-Mile Valley, the men left the trailer and the girls, waved goodbye, and headed for their field in the Cariboo. We experienced a sinking feeling as we were "plunked" in unknown territory amongst strangers. How grateful we were for the presence of the Lord and His promises. This was the beginning of a life of adventure for me. God has proved Himself in multitudinous ways.

Norene Ford joined me as a co-worker in 1949, and we started out with The Pioneer *this time.* The Chief *was doing good service on Vancouver Island. Our car was called* The Mayflower *because she pulled the* The Pioneer *and Pilgrims along.*

While travelling on B.C.'s mountain roads and highways, I had many experiences of the Lord's help in time of need. A real test of the The Pioneer *was during work up the Coast at the Powell River area. I was on my own taking the trailer*

Chapter 12—British Columbia

across the Agamemnon Channel by ferry. On reaching the ferry terminal at Saltry Bay, the cars began to unload. I started off with a steep hill in front of me. The Pioneer *had no brakes, which wasn't against the law then, and the car refused to go any further. What could I do? The emergency brake wouldn't hold the car and the trailer. The rest of the traffic just went "round me and over the hill." How I cried to the Lord.* Perhaps the ferry hasn't gone, *I thought, so I tooted and tooted the horn. It seemed a hopeless situation. But no, praise God, a ferry officer came up and asked if I was having trouble.*

He said, "If you can hold on a little longer, I'm off duty now and, although I don't usually have my car here, I do today. I'll help pull you up." How I praised God for His goodness.

The Pioneer finally had to be taken off the road as the need for brakes was enforced, and a Terry Rambler was purchased by the Mission. By this time we had advanced to a '56 Pontiac. The Pontiac pulled the trailer many miles, going into towns, villages and farming communities.

In the fall of 1965, Marie McCarroll joined me. We started out in a very unresponsive area with only a handful of children attending and the temptation was to discouragement. But our next move took us up to Malakwa in the Okanagan Valley where on the first day sixty-eight children came running down from school to the Community Church. We thought revival had begun! Down through the years we worked in this place and, praise God, souls have been saved.

These days have been the most thrilling days of my life. Counselling has been such a tremendous blessing. When people are under conviction of sin and looking to God for deliverance, it is a joy to help them with what human help they need. Many people are being saved. It is only the beginning, but a wonderful one. We need to pray for the healing of our land.

The Lord is sweeping through the Valley. May we yet see this movement becoming a Dominion-wide awakening.

It is impossible to write in detail all the way the Lord has led me. Suffice to add that for three years Pamela Klavet, from Toronto, and I laboured together, then Joyce Walsh, a Pilgrim from Ireland, and later still Janice du Toit (nee Russel), whose father was a pillar of strength to the MacFarlanes in the early days.

Through the years God has raised up wonderful, faithful prayer warriors and friends. Often we had our car loaded with canned goods, fruit, vegetables and meat. We fail to fit the description in the hymn: "Speed unburdened Pilgrims, glad, empty-handed, free...." We praise God for every provision and can say from the depths of our hearts "The Lord is my Shepherd; I shall not want."

* * * * *

After almost thirty years of hands-on and pioneering leadership in British Columbia, William and Jean MacFarlane faced retirement. For their replacement, God was preparing a young couple to follow in their footsteps, Ken and Louise Clipsham. Ken related his testimony:

I shall be eternally grateful to God for having directed me to the Faith Mission (in Canada) as a sphere of labour during the spring and summer of 1955. I had been attending the Vancouver Bible Institute (V.B.I.) during the previous fall and winter and felt I should begin to serve the Lord in some way during the summer months.

On being informed that V.B.I. would not be re-opening in the fall, I asked God, "Where shall I go? What shall I do?" One day I asked Mr. MacFarlane, the B.C. District

Superintendent of the Faith Mission, if he had any suggestions where I may go to Bible school. His reply came as if he were suggesting a place across the street, when he said, "What about the Faith Mission in Edinburgh?" So, to Scotland it was!

At the end of my training there, and after some experience with the Faith Mission in Scotland, England, and Ireland, I returned to Canada in April 1958 and started work on Vancouver Island. "Mr. Mac," as Mr. MacFarlane was fondly addressed most often, took me over and introduced me to many friends of the Mission there. He then returned to Vancouver.

Sooke was the first place I tackled. What does a person without talents and gifts do? He can tell others what Christ has done for him, and that He can do the same for them. So, visiting was the main thrust for the first few weeks, besides gathering the Christians for cottage meetings. Mr. Mac joined me for the actual preaching meetings and further visitation. Many of the Christians faithfully supported us. It will be revealed in eternity what good was accomplished in those days.

Ken moved to several locations in the Mission's work, all the while gaining valuable experience for the role the Lord would have him fill. He worked at the ten-day Bible Club in the greater Victoria area and then finished that summer at Crescent Beach.

After nine months of evangelism in Nova Scotia and assisting at Wasaga Beach services, he returned to B.C. in the fall of 1960.

Ken also went to the Kootenays where he stayed in the Presbyterian manse. From there he visited every home in around Slocan, Silverton, New Denver, and Roseberry. Further time was spent serving God at Christina Lake, Beaverdell, and Burton before returning to the B.C. headquarters to work in Lower Mainland.

During the winter, Ken hired a trailer and missioned in Courtenay, Bowser and the Sayward-Kelsey Bay area. He summed up all this time by saying, "Our hope and trust is in the Lord that much good may come out of all the going forth in His Name Who is worthy to receive all the praise."

* * * * *

Before she was married, Louise Clipsham (nee Wilson) had left her home in Southern Ireland to join the Faith Mission (in Canada). Initially, she was designated to work with Cathie Macauley in B.C. Soon she was visiting homes and farms with Cathie and conducting missions for children and adults.

In Vancouver, on September 15, 1962, Ken and Louise were married in the presence of their Faith Mission colleagues. A twenty-eight foot long trailer was supplied for them, and for the next six years that was their home on wheels. They travelled the length and breadth of Vancouver Island missioning and witnessing for the Saviour.

These pioneers, Pilgrims, and auxiliaries ploughed the ground, sowed the Seed and the Lord of the Harvest gave the increase.

CHAPTER 13

Maritime Ministry

Ken and Nellie Buchanan's life and ministry had a significant influence on the Faith Mission (in Canada) and United Kingdom. Ken was born in Ontario, and early in his Christian life, he heard God's call to fulltime Christian ministry. Through the prayerful influence of the General Director, Mr. Wallace, Ken studied at Faith Mission Bible College in Toronto and became one its earliest graduates.

As Faith Mission workers, Ken and Nellie went to Nova Scotia where, through their ministry during their first three years, over two hundred and seventy people professed faith in Jesus Christ. At times conditions were rough and afforded few human comforts. However, they experienced a touch of revival while in Nova Scotia. At times the presence of God was so real that strangers travelling through one particular area suddenly became convicted of their sin. Ken wrote of their time in the Canadian Maritimes:

The Pioneer experiences linked with the opening of the Maritime District are somewhat fascinating to recall—yes, and many of them precious experiences as well. In May 1951, my wife and I reached northern Nova Scotia where we were to plough and sow and sometimes reap. We travelled east in our '48 Dodge. Inside, and on the top carrier, was our tent, folding table, chairs and cots. At our first camp in Nova Scotia, the ice formed in the water pail. As we continued, we soon made intimate acquaintance with black flies and mosquitoes. Nell's first cupboard was an orange crate nailed to a tree.

The awareness that God was with us was confirmed as we prospected for openings for meetings in Cumberland County, where we were destined to form many lasting friendships and to see the salvation of God come to many lives. In the mining town of Spring Hill, we met an aged Nazarene minister. After telling him what we had in mind, he asked, "Why don't you go to Wyvern?" So Wyvern it was. We secured the use of the Community Church and set out to visit the people of this country district.

I remember our introduction to the area very clearly. In response to my knock on a farmhouse door, an elderly lady answered and listened to my story. Her eyes grew wide with surprise. "You want to hold meetings in Wyvern? T'won't do a bit of good. Nobody'll come."

The good lady waxed eloquent as she made a verbal reconnaissance of the community making a brief mention of the inhabitants of each house in rather discouraging terms. She terminated, saying, "Then, of course, there's old John up on the hill. He'll never come. If that man ever went to church the roof would fall down on him. And there is my husband; he won't go anywhere near your meetings. I've prayed for him for more than forty years, and he gets meaner every day! Meetings around here won't do no good."

In spite of her objections, the lady was interested. She permitted us to camp on her land and later extended to us the hospitality of the farmhouse.

We gave ourselves to prayer, and God began to work in visible ways. A woman consented to attend the meetings and

Chapter 13—Maritime Ministry

to play the organ, so we were sure of a congregation of at least one! We held meetings nightly in the church and daily in a nearby school.

Very few attended at first, but interest was kindled as the Spirit of God moved. Our friend's predictions were not fulfilled. People did come to the church. Old John from up on the hill also came, and the roof didn't fall in on him. Then came that memorable night when everything broke up. I have kept the notes of the sermon I preached that night just as a memento. I blush every time I read them and say to myself, "Did I ever preach anything as bad as that?"

It wasn't the sermon. The Holy Spirit suddenly fell on the meeting. I don't remember making any appeal, but it just seemed that, all at once, a lot of people were at the front praying. I remember a husband who had been prayed for for over forty years. He was kneeling at an old bench, and his tears made a pool on the seat before him. How wonderfully the Lord saved that man that night. He later became the teacher of a boys' class in the newly formed Sunday school. His wife became the superintendent. Concerning that class, a person in the community remarked, "If those boys never hear a thing in that Sunday school, they'll get a sermon every time they go by looking at the man who is their teacher and remembering the man he used to be."

Windam Hill is ten miles' distance from Wyvern. Here we secured the use of the schoolhouse for the mission and permission to camp in the grounds. As the work developed, we were again offered hospitality by a local farmer and his wife. Again we gave ourselves to prayer.

Interest in the community was limited, and we began in a small way. I remember well the first convert of that mission. She was a woman who had already attended three meetings *before she came to Christ. She had heard three sermons; one on "The Christian Home," one on "Salvation," and another "Hell." When I gave a brief appeal at the close of the meeting, this woman raised her head and looked at me straight in the eye. She then lifted her hand, indicating her intention to trust the Lord. She was wonderfully saved that night. She was a transformed person and manifestly had a remarkable understanding of the things of God.*

Ken told of a married couple who, during the mission at Windam Hill, packed a picnic and went to the beach. When it was time to have their lunch and they had everything set out, the husband and wife could not eat. Both of them felt constrained to pack up everything, return to their car, and head to the Gospel meeting. They arrived a little late, but both of them trusted Christ as Saviour at the meeting.

Afterward, Ken discovered something about that incident. While in Nova Scotia, it was his practice to go out into the bush and pray before the meetings until he knew he had got through to God. Later, when this couple shared their story with Ken, he discovered that it was at the very moment when he got through to God in the bush that conviction so gripped the couple that they had to leave their picnic and head for the meeting.

Many people found peace with God during the Buchanans' mission in Windham Hill, and a Prayer Union was established there. During the second mission in the town, one meeting, in particular, was memorable. Not only was every seat taken, including the extra ones, but people were standing all around the room. Numerous people had come from the surrounding rural areas. The man who hosted Ken and Nellie said to Ken, "Brother, this is revival." Ken said that although he would not call it a revival there was no doubt that the Spirit of God was moving in the district. Ken wrote:

Chapter 13—Maritime Ministry

I look back over those places we missioned in those early years in the Maritime Provinces, Westchester, Greenville, Wentworth and much more. It is possible to clearly trace the guiding hand of God over those years. In His goodness, considerable numbers entered into the safety of the Ark that is Christ.

A report at the end of 1954 reads:

Fifty missions have been conducted since the Faith Mission arrived in the Maritimes three years ago, as well as many occasional meetings. Some 132 adults have professed conversion besides 140 children. We held our second semi-annual conference in Oxford. Currently, we are ploughing the ground and sowing God's Word in Kimberly where there are around eighteen homes. Our first mission here is a softening up process and preparatory for a return visit.

As we continue our visits, we discover before long that sin abounds. Unmarried men and women live together. Even women cannot keep their speech free from occasional oaths when conversing with a Christian worker. Enmity amongst neighbours amounts to venomous hatred in some cases. What is perhaps most appalling is the utter absence of any consciousness of sin or spiritual need.

One man tells us he hasn't time to attend Christian meetings, but that one day he must find time to die. But he doesn't come. In the minds of these people there is no distinction between "being good" and "being saved" or between "conversion" and "churchgoing." However, we seek to bring the claims of Christ to all the community, whether they attend the meetings or not. We pray that before we close there may be fruit that will remain.

As we stop at a well-kept farmhouse, we hear the fierce barking of a large dog and are glad to find that he is securely tied. Approaching the house I come upon an old man busily sharpening a huge butcher knife. He has his back to me.

"That's a deadly looking weapon you have there," I remark to get his attention. He spins round and inquires in broken English what I am there for. I begin to tell him about the meetings, but he interrupts in his native tongue in a tirade about the base dealings of the priests that he witnessed in his European homeland before he came to Canada forty years ago. As his talk proceeds, his emotion and excitement grow. He keeps brandishing his knife before my face for effect, often slapping my arm with the back of the blade to emphasize his point.

Suddenly his wife appears at the door and calls out to him, "Aw, shut up!" The lady launches into another verbal tirade that sends her husband slinking around the corner of the house. She then makes an apology to me for her husband, explaining how he became embittered through suffering injustice back in his homeland.

There are many families of foreign extraction in the Maritimes. They are not easy to win for Christ. Often they are bitter against all religion and their ignorance of English is a barrier. Seldom will they ever attend even one service.

We keep on ploughing.

Chapter 14

Nova Scotia Blessings

The pioneering leadership of Ken and Nellie Buchanan in the Maritime provinces forged the way for other Faith Mission workers to join them in the work. Through balmy summers and cold and wet winters, devoted men and women steadfastly missioned, in season, out of season, sowing the Word of God.

Ken Buchanan continued to give reports of how the work progressed:

> *Many Pilgrims came to help in this district and although they usually stay for a relatively short time, each one has made a definite contribution in fulfilling God's gracious purpose. No account of the Maritime saga would be complete without recording the invaluable assistance of Ruth Weatherby and Eva Middleton. Ruth came to us about the time of the birth of our second daughter, Joan. Her fellowship and prayer ministry was a tremendous strength to us. It would require another book to relate about her giving and of her "labours oft." Ruth certainly has large and basic holdings in the Maritime enterprise.*
>
> *I first met Eva Middleton on Vancouver Island. She was on the staff of the Indian Residential School at Alberni. Later Miss Middleton spent two extensive periods of time with us in*

Nova Scotia. Faith and Joan, our daughters, referred to her affectionately as "Miggle." She also was a great help and encouragement in those days.

After a little more than four years in the Maritimes, the Faith Mission purchased a house in Oxford as our Maritime Headquarters. We had been renting that particular house for about a year with an option to buy it. Although it was a hundred years old, it was a fine, spacious house in good repair. One feature of this house was that it had a huge old woodburning furnace. It consumed such huge logs that to expect the women to "fire" it on any long-term basis while the men were away on missions was out of the question. This little matter of the furnace proved to be a focal point in securing the house as a headquarters.

About mid-summer, a friend offered to sell us a large supply of wood at a generously reduced price. This brought the onus of decision squarely upon us. We had to do the expedient thing and accept the firewood, or else take a stand of faith that the house would be bought by the Mission and an oil furnace installed. A fund for the Maritime District had been started in Toronto, but we had no idea how much was in it. Neither did we know what the house would cost. So we did what we always do at every roadblock and every crossroads; we had a prayer meeting.

After that prayer time we, my wife and I, Miss Weatherby and Brother Lund, were agreed that the Lord's will was that the Mission should secure the house. So, accordingly, we turned down the enticing offer of the cheap firewood.

For some months we believed that the house that we were renting was the place of God's choice for us. Mr. Wallace, our Mission Director, shared this conviction with us since he visited the district.

Chapter 14—Nova Scotia Blessings

In November, 1955 the house became Faith Mission property. There stood our Maritime Headquarters, debt free. How we praised God.

I wish to pay tribute to my wife's patience in putting up with primitive conditions during those earlier years. She did not complain when there was only a tent, or when we lived that first winter in two rented rooms, one above the other, together with the brothers Ohi and Edey. I was glad for her sake when the headquarters was obtained.

One feature that remains in clear remembrance was our first campaign at Kingston, Nova Scotia. It was a dual effort with meetings each day for the Academy students and each night in the church, which was one of a number of Independent Baptist Churches in the Annapolis Valley. It was to be a three-week mission.

Preceding this campaign I had been constrained to spend three days in prayer and fasting, taking only an evening meal. As I reached Kingston, it was soon evident that God was in the midst. After a week of preaching, the first invitation was given, and twenty-eight people moved forward to the front of the church to seek the Lord for various needs. At least one young man who sought the Lord that night was observed to be trembling greatly under the convicting power of the Divine Spirit.

From that point onwards there were daily conversions in the Academy as well as in the church. A number of the Lord's people also trusted Him for full salvation. It was one of those very precious visitations, which are recalled with much thanksgiving to God.

Several years later, while my wife and I were on the staff of the Prairie Bible Institute, I flew to Belleville, Ontario, for a special Youth for Christ rally. One incident I still remember

101

was an encouragement: a tall, redheaded young man came up to me and said, "I'm sure you don't know me."

When I admitted that I didn't, he continued, "I was converted as a young boy during your mission down in Kingston." At the time when he introduced himself to me, he had become a leader in Christian work among young people.

Our debt to those who give themselves to prayer on behalf of the Maritime adventure is very great. We thank God from our hearts for all such friends. We in the District found that without such strenuous and sacrificial praying, we were unable to make any impact or progress.

Here is another report from 1954:

The dawn of 1954 finds us in the thick of the fight. Strong counter-attacks by the enemy have been felt in many ways. The enemy knows how to strike through the physical, the mental, as well as the spiritual channels. We would challenge all who read this letter to set themselves, together with us, to resist the usurping foe as never before; to discipline themselves, by all means, to make this present year a glorious revival year. Let us adopt a maximum of David Livingstone, "I will go anywhere provided it is forward." It has been well said, "In revolution, victory lies with the most abandoned." That is a clever revolution! Surely, Satan has held his fearful sway too long! Let us rally 'round our rejected and rightful Sovereign, to Whom all belong by right of creation, and by purchase of blood. Let us abandon ourselves to the war to bring in His Kingdom.

From our house in Oxford we were able to reach out with the glorious Gospel into many parts of Nova Scotia, and to a lesser extent, into the adjacent New Brunswick and also into Prince Edward Island, nine miles across the water.

Chapter 14—Nova Scotia Blessings

The Rev. and Mrs. Ken Buchanan served with the Faith Mission (in Canada) for fourteen years. When leaving Nova Scotia in 1960 for Alberta, Ken Buchanan wrote:

We are saying our farewells these days to the many friends in the Maritimes whom we have come to know and love. We feel highly privileged to have worked in their midst these nine years. And, humanly speaking, it is not without regret that we take leave of them. But we feel that the time for change has come. We expect to leave Oxford in a few days time. Brother Argyle and Miss Irene Smith will be united in marriage soon. This fall they will be taking over the Maritime District.

The Buchanans were invited to move to Alberta to help open the Mission's work in Western Canada. While there, Ken became more and more involved in the Prairie Bible Institute at Three Hills, Alberta, until he eventually joined the college staff after fourteen years with the Mission.

During one of his visits to Canada, Rev. Duncan Campbell, who was Principal of the Faith Mission Bible School in Edinburgh, Scotland, was invited to speak at Prairie Bible Institute. In August 1966, Mr. Campbell felt led to ask Ken to consider moving to Scotland to take over his position as Bible College Principal. The summer of the following year, the Buchanan family uprooted from Alberta and moved to Edinburgh.

Besides heading up the Faith Mission Bible School for ten years, he was Editor of the Mission's magazine, *Bright Words,* for six years. He ministered in Faith Mission conferences and rallies all over the United Kingdom and was often in demand to preach in many churches.

The impact of Ken Buchanan's life and Bible ministry on students while in Edinburgh was immeasurable. He was outstanding both in the lecture room and the prayer room. The students were greatly influenced by his Friday morning prayer meetings and the occasional half night of prayer. Those who heard Ken pray will never forget how he would lay hold of the promises of God in prayer. John Bennett, one of the students at that time, said that when Ken prayed, he felt as if Hell trembled and the power of God was released.

In 1977, Ken and his family returned to Canada where he spent the next twelve years pastoring a church. In 1989 he responded positively to an invitation to become the General Director of the Faith Mission (in Canada). Sadly, that time was cut short after only six months when he accidently drowned while on vacation in Florida.

With the tragedy of Ken Buchanan's sudden death in 1990, the Faith Mission had lost its second Director in two years. At the end of his last contribution to the Canadian Pilgrim newsletter, he wrote,

> *Let me say something to you (and to myself), about the approaching New Year. Every challenge can have one of at least two effects on us. If we view it with doubt, it becomes a burden. If we view it with faith, it becomes an opportunity. How true this was to our experiences in the past year.*

Around 1995, John Bennett joined Raymond Thompson for a tour of Nova Scotia. A local Christian who had been very involved in meetings with Ken and Nellie Buchanan introduced them to people who had been converted or influenced through the Buchanans. John Bennett reported about the following trip:

> *I will never forget as we drove along a country road, this local Christian friend said, "Take note of this spot. During the mission everyone who crossed over this invisible line on the road suddenly became aware of the presence of God. God's presence was real everywhere within a certain radius."*

Chapter 14—Nova Scotia Blessings

I was immediately reminded of similar stories Duncan Campbell had shared with us of how the presence of God fell on communities in Scotland.

The heart cry of the Faith Mission (in Canada) is for a manifestation of the presence of God. It has been a hallmark of many evangelistic missions and spiritual retreats. The presence of God makes the feast; not our power, not our ability, or our knowledge that will move hardened sinners to repentance. The story of the Faith Mission (in Canada) would be empty and void if it were not for the presence of God.

CHAPTER 15

Canadian Challenge Today

John and Isabel Bennett have been giving leadership to the Faith Mission (in Canada) since 1992. As General Director of the Mission in Canada, John looks back with gratitude for all that God has done during these last ninety years: thousands of souls have been saved, countless numbers of believers have been blessed, churches and mission fellowships have been enriched, and through these decades, a multitude of dedicated Christian workers have served God in the ranks of the Mission.

John's gratitude for all that God has done in the past is mingled with longings and passionate desires to see God sweep through Canada in this generation with a Heaven-sent revival. It is the need of the hour. It is the prayer of his heart.

It is also with thanksgiving that John and Isabel recollect their personal testimonies of how they came to Christ and then how God led them to Canada. John writes first:

> *Because my parents and most of my siblings were converted through the ministry of the Faith Mission in Ireland, I also attended many Faith Mission meetings when I was a child. I trusted Jesus to save me at one of these kids' meetings when I was seven years old. I attended many Faith Mission evangelistic missions, Mission conferences, and the weekly Prayer*

Union, which was held in my parents' home, with the result that I received a good grounding in the Christian faith.

I left school just before my fifteenth birthday to join my parents on the family farm. Although I was a Christian, I was challenged about my lack of power to witness to others about Christ. I longed to be able to share my faith but felt so inadequate.

June 29th, 1963 was a red-letter day for me. On that day I listened to a preacher expound Acts 1:8: "You will receive power after the Holy Spirit is come upon you, and you will be witnesses unto Me in Jerusalem, Judea and to the uttermost parts of the earth." *As he spoke, I became convicted of sin in my life that was hindering the Holy Spirit. On that day I confessed my sin to God and surrendered my life wholly to the control of the Holy Spirit, trusting God to cleanse and fill me with His Spirit. Little did I know that step would lead to God calling me from the farm and eventually taking us to Canada.*

By the time I was nineteen years old, I had a growing conviction that farming was not God's plan for my life. Although I loved farming, the inner conviction that God was calling me kept growing. I fought against it for some time by making lots of excuses and genuinely believed they were legitimate reasons: my dad needs me, I do not have enough education, I am too shy ever to be a public speaker. *All this was true, but I am thankful that God paid no attention to any of them. He used the death of some animals on the farm to make me see that if I stayed out of the will of God, I would be a hindrance and not a help to my family.*

God spoke to me and confirmed His call on my life through the Scriptures in 1 Corinthians 1:26-29, where God said He has chosen the weak things of this world so that no flesh should glory in His presence. Again, by reading 1 Corinthians 4:15, the Lord confirmed my call to the Faith Mission: "For though

CHAPTER 15—CANADIAN CHALLENGE TODAY

you have ten thousand instructors in Christ, yet have you not many fathers: for in Christ Jesus I have begotten you through the Gospel, therefore be followers of me."

It was in January 1968 that I left home for the Faith Mission Bible College in Edinburgh, Scotland. Although I enjoyed my time there, I cannot say those were easy years, but the lessons learned during that period have been invaluable to me ever since. I learned that Jesus Christ is Lord and is adequate for all I needed in every circumstance I might encounter. I also discovered that yesterday's experiences and blessings are not sufficient for today. Our experience of God must be up to date, for it is too easy to become stagnant.

I am glad that I also learned that God is the great Provider and His promises to supply all our needs can be trusted. I proved this to be true through a very practical experience. It was coming near time to go home from the Bible college, and that meant I needed money to travel by bus, sea ferry, and train from Edinburgh to Dublin. My dad had told me if I ever needed money I just had to let him know. I was about to write a letter to him when I became convicted that I was trusting in my earthly father and not in my Heavenly Father. That day I told God that from then on I would trust Him alone. That is when the test came. The date for departure was fast approaching, and I had only one ten-shilling note (about 80 Canadian cents). That only compounded the problem for I had made a covenant with God that I would put ten shillings into the weekly missionary offering. What was I to do? I felt I must honour my commitment to God even though that would leave me with nothing. It certainly was a test of faith for me, but God is faithful, and before I needed to travel, sufficient money came to cover the full fare all the way to Dublin. I was praising God.

Although God had provided my fare, I did not expect that the trip home would be so eventful. The Lord allowed the ferry to be late, and this resulted in me missing my place on the Dublin train. I therefore had to spend some of my precious train-fare money to travel to an aunt where I stayed overnight. Next morning, my aunt gave me some money to buy food. This unexpected gift relieved the pressure as I now had enough for the train ticket with a little to spare. I did not spend it on food.

On arrival in the Dublin Station, there was a call for me to go to the information desk. The attendant gave me a message to get the bus to a local town where my family would meet me. After I had purchased that bus ticket, I had exactly one penny left. That day I learned that God knew precisely what I needed and He also knew all the diversions along the road before I met them.

After forty-nine years of trusting God alone to supply my personal needs, the needs of our family, and the needs of the Mission, God has not once failed to keep His promise.

After college, I had the privilege of working with the Faith Mission in England, Ireland, and Scotland. Isabel and I were married on July 9, 1976. Since that day, Isabel has been a pillar of strength to me. Her vision has shaped much of what we have done together, both in the United Kingdom, in Ireland, and in Canada. God also blessed our home with three sons.

In 1990 we received an invitation to join the Faith Mission team in Canada. After praying and asking God to show us if this was His will, we received no leading to go, so we felt we had to decline the offer. A year later the invitation was renewed, and this time I asked God for a specific verse. The answer came in Psalm 107:7: "He led them forth by the right way." *God had used this verse earlier in my life*

Chapter 15—Canadian Challenge Today

when I was about to graduate from Bible college. I knew the Mission would soon locate me in some part of the United Kingdom or Ireland. I became anxious about this because I wondered: What would happen if the Mission sent me someplace that God did not want me to be?

The Lord gave me peace through the same verse: "He led them forth by the right way." *It was then I realized my life was not in the hands of the Faith Mission Council, but in God's hands and I could trust Him.*

As we were praying about Canada, I wondered when and how God would give me this verse. I attended Faith Mission board meetings in Scotland and Canada, but there was no word from God. While in Canada meeting with the board, Isabel phoned to say there was a verse on her mind and wondered if it was the verse I had asked of God. I had not mentioned anything to her about the verse for which I had been waiting. I asked Isabel not to tell me. I said that if God wants us in Canada, He will make it very clear.

One morning as we were both having our quiet times with God, Isabel suddenly spoke up and said, "There is that verse I have had on my mind."

This time I asked what it was. Isabel read Psalm 107:7 out loud, "He led them forth by the right way." *I could hardly believe it, but I knew we had the final confirmation. God, in His goodness, gave us another encouragement. With all medical and other related costs including flights, we needed over £5,000. We promised God we would not tell anyone of this need but wholly trust in Him.*

Exactly two weeks before we flew to Canada, after every penny had been supplied, the flow of financial income suddenly dried up. God had given us all that we needed without a surplus.

Our family settled quickly in Canada. Stephen, our oldest son, and his wife, Kara, live in British Columbia. Jonathan and his wife, Katie, live in Ontario as do our youngest son Andrew and his wife, Michelle. We are delighted to have six Canadian grandchildren.

Sometimes people ask us, "What would you do if you had your life to live over again?" I think I could honestly say, "I would do exactly the same again." The exception being that on the second time around, I hope I would be more faithful, more believing, more diligent in prayer and Bible study, and more robust in witnessing for Christ. I would also hope that people would see more of God and less of me.

Chapter 16

No Secret What God Can Do

Every conversion is a miracle of immense mercy, a trophy of amazing grace, and a testimony to the dynamic power of the Gospel of Jesus Christ. Isabel Bennett is the wife of John Bennett, the General Director of the Faith Mission (in Canada). The story of her coming to Jesus Christ certainly fits the definition of a genuine and radical conversion.

St. Andrews is one of the most famous and picturesque cities in Scotland. Besides being universally recognized as the home of golf and renowned for its famous course and greens, the city also has the oldest English-speaking university in the world where current British Royals have studied. It was also in St. Andrews that the saintly Samuel Rutherford ministered the Word of God and where many Scottish Covenanters were martyred for their faith and love for Christ.

Moreover, this famous city was the birthplace of Isabel Bennett, who plays a vital part in serving alongside her husband John in leading the work of the Faith Mission (in Canada). Isabel's story is best told in her own words, in which you can trace God's grace and providence in her life:

Childhood

I was born into the Simpson family, a family that had no claim to fame, fortune, or royalty and most certainly was not a "faith" family. As an innocent and helpless baby, I had no knowledge of what life was all about or what it was going to look like. I did hear the name of Jesus and God repeated many times, but in a derogative manner. By today's standards, we would be classed as a low income and dysfunctional family. We lived in a one-room home. My father worked hard to keep food on the table and clothes on our backs, but my mother was an alcoholic who was more often under the influence of liquor than sober. When she was intoxicated, she became a husband abuser, both physically and verbally. Money that was needed for food was used to satisfy her alcoholic addiction. It didn't help that there was a public house on the corner of our street and another just a block away. Mother spent most of her time in these dens as a bar waitress and a singer.

Needless to say, my childhood memories are not of happiness, safety, security, or of a loving home. In fact, it was the complete opposite. There are many dark pictures stored in my memory bank, with only a few happy exceptions that I treasure. My best memories were of my loving grandparents who cared enough to try to make me happy and content. Suffice to say that from a very early age, I knew sexual and verbal abuse as well as obnoxious bullying. It was not uncommon for me to experience hunger or witness scenes of violence at home.

By the time I reached five years of age, my father, having taken all the abuse he could, left home. He was the only person who had made home life bearable for me, but now he was gone. He had been my rock and was always there to care for us.

Chapter 16—No Secret What God Can Do

A scene that is etched in my memory is a day coming home from school for lunch to an empty house and no one to take care of my temporal needs. I found my nine-month-old baby sister crying, soiled and hungry. Many school lunch-hour breaks were spent taking care of my sister's needs as best as I knew how while my mother was caring for her alcohol addiction. It was around this time that my sister was placed in a children's home.

Divorce papers were filed, and after the divorce was finalized, my father was awarded full custody of my sister and I. I later learned a Bible verse in Psalm 27:10: "When my father and mother forsake me, then the Lord will take me up." *I am glad that I was not entirely abandoned.*

Dad took me to live with him, but he did not have steady employment or a permanent home. That meant we had to move around from one place to another without any stability at home or in school.

My mother had visitation rights and one night at an arranged meeting place; there was to be a "handing over" from my father to my mother. When they met, there was another heated argument. This ended with one of them walking away in one direction and the other in the opposite direction. I was left cowering in a hole in a hedge, scared of the darkness and what was happening. On that night I felt abandoned by both of my parents.

While I was cowering under the hedge, a policeman found me. As a result, I began an adventure of family-care swapping until I ended up again in my mother's care with her live-in boyfriend, of which she had many. Once again the abuses resumed, and they got even worse to the point of near strangulation.

One day my mother packed my clothes and landed me at the door of my retired paternal grandparents. She told them I was their son's responsibility and since he wasn't around, she didn't want the responsibility of me anymore. Once again I was abandoned, but still had not discovered that "When my father and mother forsake me, then the Lord will take me up."

My grandparents took care of me as best they could during the summer holidays from school, but their home did not have the necessary facilities to care for a seven-year-old girl. They were annoyed when they saw how I was abused and bullied by children in their neighbourhood. I still bear the scars of physical injuries I suffered from those kids. My grandparents were so heartbroken they had no choice but to call the child services and they placed me in a foster home.

Although this was not a Christian home, God was looking out for me. Nothing much changed in that foster home. I was provided for, clothed, fed, but abuses continued. Nevertheless, there was one good thing that happened. On my first Saturday there, I was taken out to purchase a wardrobe of new clothes. Some of these were the prettiest dresses I had ever seen. On the following day, I got dressed up in what was known as "my Sunday best." My foster parents' daughter and son, who were Christians, took me to Sunday school. Pretty clothes, Sunday school, and church services were all new to me, but I felt that I looked as pretty as a princess and did not want to ask questions about it all. God was taking care of me.

CONVERTED

I was about to go on another adventure, but this time with God. Sunday school was totally different from anything I had known; singing, praying memorizing Scripture, and stories from the Bible. What I loved best was being told that Jesus loved me. It was that love that drew my young heart to the

Chapter 16—No Secret What God Can Do

Saviour. Just to know that I was loved and that Jesus would never leave me or forsake me. This was a sweet balm to a young child whose emotions were all over the place. I was glad to learn that I would always be loved and never abandoned.

The Holy Spirit was at work in my life, preparing me for the time He would draw me to Jesus. I knew all about Jesus and His love for me, but I was still not his child. By this time, under the ministry of the Faith Mission, my foster parents had become Christians.

When I was twelve years old, we moved from our village to the town of Glenrothes where we started to attend a Baptist church. There I discovered that knowing about Jesus was not enough; Sunday school, church attendance and young people's meetings and all my head knowledge of Jesus were not sufficient. I needed a heart transformation.

God wasn't interested in my goodness, whatever that was. The Holy Spirit convicted me of my sin and challenged me through His Word: "For God so loved the world…." He chose me, and I embraced Jesus. The Son of God became my Saviour. I now belonged to the family of God. I became a daughter of THE KING.

Called

I was really taken aback when I discovered that the Holy Spirit was working out His plan and purpose for my life. At seventeen years old, I had my plans, and I thought I knew what I was going to do with my life. I wanted to become a nurse, meet a boyfriend, eventually get married and have my own family.

One night, in a Faith Mission prayer meeting at a summer beach outreach, God spoke to me, "Isabel, I have other plans for you."

I was challenged again that night as I had been a few years previously at a Stephen Olford Crusade in Edinburgh, Scotland. After Dr. Olford had preached on "Handing Your Life Fully and Totally over to God," I stood as an act of surrender with many other young people as we sang, "Follow Him, Follow Him, Yield your life to Him...Give to Him complete control of body and of soul." I might have been caught up in the emotional atmosphere of that evening, but I did mean it at the time. However, it was on the night of the Faith Mission prayer meeting that I recognized I needed to go through with the vow I had made to God. I sincerely surrendered my all to Him.

I did not fully know what surrender would entail until I realized that God was asking me to leave my employment and my ambitions and go to the Faith Mission Bible College in Edinburgh. I questioned, "Lord, are You sure?"

Because my education had taken me through thirteen public schools and two secondary schools, I was sure that no Bible college would ever accept me. I thought, My best friend would be a better choice. She has a better education and considerable ability, but who am I?

God's reply hit me with a double whammy; "Do you remember what you said to Me in the Stephen Olford Crusade meeting?"

Called by God to such a high and holy calling? I was frightened, inadequate, a small non-educated girl who was feeling unclean and unworthy. I needed a word from God to confirm that this call was definitely from Him.

I vividly remember how the confirmation came. While I was in my bedroom seeking God for a word from Him, my foster mother entered with a letter for me. I thought, A letter? No one writes to me.

Chapter 16—No Secret What God Can Do

The letter was from a young man with whom I was friendly but not in a relationship. I had shared with him the struggle I was having so he felt prompted to mail a letter to me, even though he only lived down the road.

I opened the letter, and what caught my eye was a Scripture that he had written to encourage me: "Fear thou not for I am with thee, don't be dismayed for I am your God. I will strengthen you; I will help you, I will uphold you with my righteous right hand" *(Isaiah 41:10). The Lord was assuring me that He would not abandon me in this adventure. That was it. I felt like Martin Luther at the Diet of Worms: "Here I stand, I can do no other."*

Armed with the confidence that God had called and that He would be with me, desiring to make my life count for God, I entered the Faith Mission Bible College in 1971.

Now I look back on many stories of God's faithfulness, His many blessings and timely provisions while working with the Faith Mission as a single girl in Northern Ireland and England. For a short while I stepped out of the will of God, but in His grace and mercy, He brought me back, rebuilding that broken wall of fellowship.

God provided me with a godly and loving husband, and together we served God with the Faith Mission in the United Kingdom and Ireland for nearly twenty-five years. We have been blessed with three sons, Stephen, Jonathan, and Andrew. Even though I am not without failings, the Lord has enabled me to be a different mom from the one I had known.

Called to Canada

In 1990 John received a letter from the Faith Mission (in Canada) asking if he would prayerfully consider becoming the

General Director of the work there. You could only imagine our surprise and shock. God was rocking our boat and unsettling my comfort zone. We were extremely happy serving the Lord in Scotland, based in Edinburgh. Our boys were settled in school; our oldest son was soon to start his senior education. Life was good, and we were content with where God had placed us.

We arrived in Canada on August 26th, 1992. We can truly say that we put our hand to the plough and there was no looking back. There have been no regrets because there is no greater thrill; no greater joy than being in the centre of the will of God and there is no safer or more secure place to be.

But for the grace of God, I dread to think what my life might be like today.

CHAPTER 17

Multi Ministries

During the ninety years of the Faith Mission (in Canada), the work has developed and evolved. The message of the everlasting Gospel is forever the same, but through the decades Mission workers have learned to be flexible and adaptable to changing times and circumstances. Transportation, accessibility, and communication were very restrictive in the early pioneering days of the mission. The twenty-first century is an age of rapid development in which communication and transportation allow us to employ a variety of means to preach the Gospel and reach the lost for Christ. The Mission, therefore, still seeking first the Kingdom of God and relying on the power of the Holy Spirit, operates on many fronts to effectively communicate the Scriptures to people.

KIDS' AND YOUTH MINISTRY

As quoted earlier in this book, John Wallace, the former Director of the Faith Mission (in Canada), before he went to be with the Lord in his one hundred and fifth year, said, "If I had my life to live over again, I think I would be a children's evangelist." He gave the following reasons for his statement. Firstly, when a child is saved by

Christ, a whole life is saved for the Lord. Secondly, little children are so impressionable. Therefore, it is important to reach them before their minds are moulded and corrupted by the world and its values. The final reason for his avowal was that when a boy or girls trust Christ, it is often a door to reaching parents with the Gospel. Grace imparts grace to others.

Although John Wallace spent the major part of his life in Bible ministry and evangelism among adults, and God greatly blessed him in that ministry, he did not consider children's work as inferior or a second-rate work. According to his statement, he saw it as even more important than ministry to adults.

The vision to reach children has been clear from the inception of the Mission in 1927 when the first Faith Mission evangelists arrived in Canada. During July and August, 1928, they led a team to Wasaga Beach and the surrounding beaches to conduct meetings for kids and adults.

That ministry continued each year until 1988 when a town by-law made it illegal to preach on the beaches. The team then continued their children's outreach in the local parks. Many adults remark to us that they can trace their conversion to those beach and park meetings. The Faith Mission teams carried out similar ministries on the Crescent Beach in B.C. Furthermore, in almost every Faith Mission evangelistic campaign, children's meetings are also conducted. It is no exaggeration to say that throughout the ninety years of the Mission's history, thousands of children and youth have professed faith in Christ at various meetings.

While the message has not changed, in recent years the methods have. The Apostle Paul said that he made himself *"all things for all men that by all means, he might reach some."* He then added, *"And this I do for the Gospel's sake."* Today's workers take every opportunity to present the Gospel to kids and youth.

Chapter 17—Multi Ministries

Through the summer, most of the Mission staff are involved in teaching at Vacation Bible Schools in churches and camp ministry. Full-time workers are joined each summer by dedicated students who assist at these events. During the remainder of the year, many of the Mission workers come alongside local churches to help launch and often conduct weekly kids and youth clubs. The aim is to help organize the clubs for a limited period while training church members in the hope that these trainees will take full responsibility for their church meetings. Sometimes this can be difficult as many smaller rural churches do not have sufficient people available and willing to take on a regular club.

A constant challenge facing many pastors is finding Christians who are willing to be committed to reaching lost souls. Sadly, we live in a very self-satisfied society, even in the Christian church many are glad to know they are saved and ready for heaven, but show little or no concern for lost people around them. They know little of what Paul testified to in Romans 9 when he stated he was willing to be accursed if it meant the salvation of his fellow countrymen.

Lamentably, Canada is filled with impressionable kids, the vast majority of whom have never heard the simple Gospel message. Their minds are bombarded each day from media and in school with all kinds of humanistic, atheistic, and evolutionist teaching with no absolutes. This trend opens the door to every kind of unbiblical ideology and behaviour. By trying to ignore or bypass God's Word and the exclusiveness of the Gospel, they live as if there is no personal accountability, no moral responsibility, and no coming judgment. It is for this reason that there is an urgency to reach boys and girls before this pollution and corruption take hold. May God help us in the Canadian Faith Mission and our Christian friends to double our efforts in prayer and evangelism to reach lost children while the opportunity is still before us.

Camp Ministry

A major part of the Mission's summer outreach is taken up with four weeks of camps that are held at the Falkland Centre in B.C. Another four weeks of camps are organized at the Campbellville Centre in Ontario, and one or two other camp weeks are held in Quebec. The Mission's Winter Snow Camps are also very popular. These camping events attract young people from a variety of backgrounds; some come from good Christian homes and others from dysfunctional and non-church families, some who have heard the Gospel from birth while many kids hear the Gospel for the first time. Some arrive with hearts prepared to participate, listen and learn, while others come with sin-hardened and rebellious hearts.

All these camps are staffed by Faith Mission workers who are ably assisted by students and others who are prepared to sacrifice a week or more of their vacation to help. It is heart-warming to see counsellors and kids bonding and to sense the love these volunteers have for the children, even for those who may cause them heartbreak at times. Over the years there have been some tough camps when real spiritual battles raged. On the other hand, there have been other camps when there was a glorious outpouring of the Holy Spirit and a genuine harvest of souls.

At the Falkland Camp in B.C. during the summer of 2016, God came down in such a way that both leaders and campers were broken before Him. Some campers were saved, and others surrendered their lives to God. These experiences mark young lives for life. They also make us dissatisfied with anything less than an outpouring of God's Holy Spirit.

John Bennett, the Mission's General Director, gave a report on one particular camp in Ontario:

Some years ago at a camp in Campbellville, Ontario the spiritual battle was very real. Chapel teachers struggled to get the

Chapter 17—Multi Ministries

message across. Individual quiet times were chaotic, and the kids did not seem to be interested. Although we engaged in believing prayer through that week, nothing seemed to change. However, it was all reversed on the final evening. We gathered round the campfire to sing, in the hope that there would be some testimonies. Initially, the atmosphere was cold with no sense of freedom. It was like hitting a brick wall to get participation. Suddenly, one young man began to beat his breast and cry, "I need God, I need God."

A hush came over the whole camp, and the cloud of coldness and hardness lifted. God came down amongst us. All the leader could do was to suggest that everyone get on their knees and pray. Silently people moved away from the fire and began praying in small groups around the field. Tough teenage boys were weeping like babies. As we moved around the groups, we could sense the presence and power of God at work.

While all this was happening, the Camp Director was called to a small group of older teens that had left the field and were holding another teenager on the ground. This young man was in agony and obviously very distressed. When we asked what was wrong, another teenager answered, said, "He is not sick, it is what he was involved in before coming to camp." It became evident that there was some occult activity.

A second teenager inside the camp building was totally out of control. He ran around the room shouting, overturning chairs, and hitting out at anything in sight. The camp leader paced the grounds with that young man that night, quoting Scriptures and praying with him. The teenager later went to bed in a daze. When he left camp next day, he was still in a state of bewilderment. The camp leader said he had never seen such a manifestation of the powers of darkness. At the same time, there was such a demonstration of the power of God at the camp like they had never seen before, nor since. The leader said, "Paradoxically, it was one of the most terrible and most wonderful nights of my life."

The battle for the minds and hearts of these precious young lives is very real. When we think of them, we still ask, "Who will stand in the gap? Who will tell them of Jesus? Who will pray for them?"

YOUTH LEADERSHIP TRAINING

John Bennett continues to relate about the camp ministry:

Soon after the Campbellville Centre was purchased and summer and winter camps commenced, it became apparent that it would be beneficial to offer some leadership training to camp counsellors and others who may be involved.

During the school's mid-semester break in March 1997, we launched a week-long Youth Leadership Training program. Over the years since, a variety of subjects have been addressed: How to Study the Bible, Having a Quiet Time, The Crucified Life, Sharing Your Testimony, Teaching a Bible Story, Bible Memorization, Teaching a Memory Verse, Your Walk with God, Knowing the Will of God, Apologetics and Being a Camp Counsellor. The lessons included the biographies of several great missionary statesmen and women. The opportunity was also given for practical experience in door-to-door visitation, involvement in Vacation Bible Schools, Youth meetings in local churches, sharing in an open-air street meeting, or distribution of Gospel tracts in a local town.

A similar program is held at the Falkland Centre since the beginning of the work there, and recently the staff in Quebec introduced a related course for that province.

Chapter 17—Multi Ministries

We have been encouraged to see that many who came through the programs are in full-time Christian ministry today; some on the staff of the Faith Mission (in Canada), others serving God with other missions or as pastors and leaders in local churches.

Camp and Conference Centres

The value of Christians being able to step out of their weekly routine to spend quality time in fellowship with other believers is incalculable. It is a principle established by our Lord who invited His disciples to "*come apart and rest a while.*" God provided two camp/conference centres for the Faith Mission (in Canada): Campbellville in Ontario and Falkland in B.C. Both centres are used throughout the year for Summer and Winter Camps, Youth Leadership Training, Ladies and Men's Retreats, Thirsting for God Conferences and Christmas banquets.

When not in use by the Faith Mission, church and mission groups use the facilities for their conferences. It is impossible to calculate how many souls have been saved or how many of God's people have been brought to a place of full surrender to God at these centres. We are always hearing from people who testify how they came to Christ or how much they have been blessed through the ministry at the centres. It is so encouraging to hear people say, "There is such a sense of God in that centre." Others remark, "I don't want to leave." We often see kids crying at the end of camp because they don't want to leave. We even hear some wives say their husbands were transformed since they attended a men's retreat at one of these centres.

The conferences centres are very busy places, and the respective managers must be commended for the way they welcome groups, lend a listening ear to those who want to share their burdens and blessings. They also display a servant-like heart in their service for the Saviour.

Since purchasing these conference properties in Ontario and B.C., extensive renovations have been carried out on them. This work cost thousands of dollars that were donated to the work. It also involved hundreds of working hours, which skilled people and volunteers generously gave to ensure the upgrading and maintenance of these ministries at a minimum cost.

Thirsting for God Conferences

Soon after the founding of the Faith Mission in Scotland, John George Govan recognized the value of bringing new converts together for teaching, fellowship, and prayer. From the beginning of the Mission in Canada, the leadership has sought to follow that example. They organize rallies in key locations, bringing people from different denominations together for fellowship and deepening of their Christian lives. Guest speakers teach and challenge on subjects such as holiness of life, commitment to prayer, death to self, obedience to the Great Commission and involvement in their local churches. Following these rallies, many testify of how they have been blessed.

In recent years the Mission leadership decided on calling these annual gatherings, "Thirsting For God Conferences." Their reasons for this title are outlined as follows:

> *It is God we need. Many Christians seek the blessing when they should be seeking the Blesser. Matthew 6:33, which is one of the Mission's mottos, says,* "Seek first the Kingdom and all these things will be added unto you." *When God is in first place, everything else will fit into its rightful place.*
>
> *God promises His fullness to those who are thirsty:* "Blessed are those who hunger and thirst after righteousness;

Chapter 17—Multi Ministries

for they shall be filled." *God wants His people to thirst for Him.*

To those who are thirsty, God promises His fullness—to "send the floods on the dry ground." How conscious we are of the dry ground all around us, even at times in our own souls. If the rice fields remain dry or only moist, there will be little to harvest. The rice needs the ground to be flooded. Today, we need those floods to counter the barren and unfruitful climate that has invaded much of our Christianity.

Some rallies are convened as a one-day conference. Other meetings are held over a weekend or a week. During the conferences, the mornings are reserved for sessions of united prayer and the main conference meeting is in the evening.

John Bennett reports about these Thirsting for God Conferences:

People speak and write of the blessings they have received at these meetings and how their lives have been changed. One pastor shared how his whole ministry was revolutionized after attending a Thirsting for God Conference. A young man said he would never be the same again. Another said, "This is what I have been searching for."

Some people confessed that they had never known victory was possible in their Christian lives until they attended one of our conferences. We find that those who receive the greatest blessings at the conferences are those who are the most committed in their local churches and attend the conference's mornings of prayer. At the close of some meetings, we have seen almost the whole congregation seeking God. At such times no one wants to move, so sweet has been the presence of God.

Of course, there have been other conferences where people have resisted the Holy Spirit and leave the meeting untouched. I have concluded that indifference is one of the great hindrances to revival and blessing. When hungry, thirsty souls meet in the presence of God, they will be filled. God has promised.

One pastor wrote of how he and his church had been refreshed in God's presence at one of the Thirsting for God Conferences:

For five refreshing evenings at the beginning of November, the purifying presence of the Spirit of God visited us at Faith Baptist, Oakville. We captioned the week, "Heart-cry for a Spiritual Awakening." Throughout the week, many precious moments served to instruct our hearts regarding the power and enrichment of prevailing prayer.

I wish to express my gratitude to God for the ministry of the Word by personnel from the Faith Mission, along with others closely associated with the Mission. The gracious response of our people; the fellowship of prayer, which linked our hearts together, has given me immense encouragement, for which I praise God.

Gordon H. Phillips, Pastor

CHAPTER 18

Abounding In the Work of the Lord

Glenn and Robin Deane live in Bracebridge, one hundred and fifty kilometres north of Toronto. Glenn is a Teaching Pastor at Pinegrove Fellowship Church where he is part of a team that is exercising an effective ministry for the Lord. Before entering the settled ministry in Bracebridge, Glenn and his wife, Robin, served God with the Faith Mission (in Canada).

Glenn recalled his days of service with the Mission:

When we first embarked on our Faith Mission work in Mount Forest, Ontario, we saw little consistent work beyond one-off meetings and a roster of Sunday services. However, the Lord soon opened an unexpected door when we began taking the Word of God into public schools.

This opportunity arose after the summer work at various Vacation Bible Schools (VBS) and summer camps. We rented a neutral location to hold a VBS in our small town, the local curling club. During that week, one of our son's school teachers dropped by and, since she lived in town, she brought some treats with her. Because the teacher had been used to how many children attended the children's meeting at her local church, she arrived with enough goodies for a dozen or so children. When she saw our building packed with over eighty children, she was dumbfounded and a little embarrassed. She sheepishly ventured out to purchase some more timbits.

In September, that same teacher approached us to consider holding meetings at the school that our own children attended. She said that she had spoken to the principal and after some fine-tuning, he was agreeable for us having lunch-hour meetings. We drafted a form giving full details of what the meetings were about and asked for the parents' consent for their children to attend. We were careful to keep strict attendance records. Children who did not have permission forms were given them for their parents to sign.

Our first year was remarkable. Numbers swelled into triple digits. The only room in the school that could accommodate such numbers was the gymnasium. At first, we thought that the parental permission form would be a hindrance to children attending. Instead, it became a badge of honour. Children announced to their friends that they were allowed to go to "Kids Club," adding, "You cannot attend unless your mother says its ok." The novelty of a seemingly "secret club" caught the curiosity of the children. Dozens of them not only came, but they also stayed.

These simple meetings consisted of singing choruses, a Bible story, and a group game. Children sat on the cold floor and ate their lunch during the Bible lesson. We then had them pack up their belongings, divide into teams for games and let them burn off some energy. Prayer was paramount to keeping that many children quiet, organized and co-operative. The Lord gave us peace in those meetings, but there were occasions when we had to deal radically with a few children and have them leave the meeting. I'm glad to say those occasions were extremely rare.

At the end of the academic year, we received an invitation to the school assembly when all the school's clubs would

Chapter 18—Abounding In the Work of the Lord

be acknowledged, and children receive recognition for their various accomplishments. At the assembly, as each club was announced, the children involved, rose from sitting cross-legged on the gym floor and made their way to the front. They remained before the student body while a citation was read out about their respective achievements. There were seven or eight children in the Chess Club, a dozen from the Cross-Country Running Club, and these were followed by five or six children in the Reading Club.

Our Kids' Club was the last to be called. "Would all the children in the Kids' Club please make their way to the front." That was a moment I shall never forget. The entire floor rippled to life. We knew there would be a handful of children in each club, but when they called for the Kids' Club, well over a hundred boys and girls, more than a third of the entire student body, rose to their feet and tiptoed around the seated children to the front. A teacher sitting beside me gave me a nudge. I looked at her. She had coffee in her hand; her eyes were wide open as was her mouth. She was totally shocked and unable to believe what she was seeing. I responded with a simple shrug of my shoulders as if it were an everyday thing to have so many children in one club. There was not room enough across the front of the gym for our children to stand in a single line.

We are still not fully aware of all that God did during that season of sowing the Gospel in that school. The Lord of the Harvest gives the increase and the harvest day is in His hands. Although that Kids' Club continued for nine years, it never reached such high numbers as in that first year. The Lord also opened other doors, and before long, we were involved in clubs in five public schools in that area. It was an unprecedented season in which the Lord gave us great joy in sharing His Word among that generation.

Our summer work was filled with travel and children. One week in particular stands out. We were teaching at a children's camp in rural Ontario. The week was going well, and the Word was being received. However, one day there was an interruption. In the middle of the teaching session, the back door of the building swung open, and a child stumbled in. It was odd to see a camper arriving so late for the meeting. For a moment I wondered if the counsellors had not been keeping tabs on their campers. I continued with the meeting and ignored the disruptive noise of this boy wandering and looking for a seat. Each cabin group sat together, but this kid did not seem to find where he belonged. Finally, he sat down and soon I began the Bible story.

I was telling the story of Zacchaeus. Toward the end of the talk, I included a simple explanation of salvation and explained that if any child needed to talk about their spiritual problems, they should wait afterward.

As I was closing the meeting in prayer, a commotion started. Assuming the counsellors would deal with it, I kept on praying, but the disturbance continued. I could hear someone talking. I was hoping for silence during the prayer, but there was none. After the prayer, the children were dismissed, but I was not sure what the noise had been about. I soon learned.

The child who had wandered into the building was not a camper. His father had stopped by near the camp to visit his parents, who owned the camp facility. While there, his ten-year-old son meandered off and discovered a building full of children. He came in, found a seat, and for the first time in his life he heard the Gospel. He also was the boy who had been speaking out loudly when I was closing the meeting in prayer. His father was the wayward son of the owners of the camp and had tried to shelter his son from any spiritual influence.

Chapter 18—Abounding In the Work of the Lord

He certainly wasn't interested in passing on the faith he had grown up hearing. We know that with God, even a hard heart cannot stop the effect of parents who continually intercede for their family.

This young boy knew that some people prayed audibly, but was not aware that a person could also pray silently. While listening to the story of Zacchaeus, he came under conviction of guilt and sin. Just as the Lord had spoken to little Zacchaeus in Jericho, this kid also heard the voice of Jesus say, "Today I am coming to your house."

As I was closing in prayer, the boy had been audibly pleading with God to save him. Words cannot express how thrilled his grandparents were at the goodness of God and this answer to their prayers. The message of the Gospel had brought salvation back to their home again.

I kept in touch with that boy over the years since and today he is an adult and still walking with God. Praise God.

Pastor Glenn Deane and his wife, Robin, certainly have reason to be thankful to God for the wealth of experience they gained in taking the Gospel to children and adults in the highways and byways of rural Canada.

Chapter 19

How God Provides

The Faith Mission was founded on the principle of trusting God for every need: spiritual, financial, material and physical. Throughout its history, the Mission's policy has been not to publish financial needs or make public appeals for finance. Workers are not asked to raise guaranteed support before joining the Mission or during their time in the work. God has been faithful and honoured this stand of faith for over one hundred and thirty years since the Mission was founded in 1886. Every year the Mission has been able to meet its financial obligations. This is not in any way due to the measure of our faith. It is a testimony to God's great faithfulness.

Many years ago the Mission's Canadian Board adopted a no-debt policy, believing that if God wants us to have something, He will supply that need. Every worker is treated equally in financial support, and all are expected to exercise faith in God to meet their personal needs and the overall requirements of the Mission. When a need arises, it is made a matter of personal and corporate prayer within the Mission personnel. How thrilling it has been to see how God answers prayer and touches individuals and churches to contribute to the Lord's work in the Faith Mission.

It would be impossible to catalogue and recount all the wonderful answers to prayer over the years, but God's faithful provision has always been amazing. "Provision" is a compound word; pro indicates "beforehand, " and vision obviously means "to see." When we speak of "God's provision" it reminds us that He sees our need before it becomes apparent to us. He not only sees, but He also furnishes what He sees is necessary and what is best. We can rest confidently in His faithfulness for He is in the future and controls the future.

John Bennett recounts some of God's amazing and timely provisions.

Camp and Conference Centre in Surrey B.C.

In November, 1993 a group of interested friends met with the Mission's B.C. staff, Gerhard and Janice du Toit, and the General Director, John Bennett, to discuss issues relevant to the work in that region. During their discussions, all agreed that a permanent conference and camp centre would be an excellent addition to the ministry.

Within weeks of that meeting, a call came through asking if the Faith Mission would be interested in acquiring a beautiful centre on a seven-acre lot overlooking the Pacific Ocean in Surrey B.C. The challenge that was contingent with the inquiry was that the Mission would take responsibility for all debts on the property and agree to support a missionary doctor who would remain on her field of service for the rest of her term.

When the Mission Treasurer Ken Clipsham counted the pennies, he discovered that God had already made provision. A former Mission worker from South Africa had bequeathed a sum of South African Rand to the Mission, although we had no idea how much the legacy was worth. In addition to that legacy, some years earlier, several friends in Ontario had donated gifts to the Mission in the hope that one day we would be able to have a camp/conference centre. That money had been deposited in a special Camp Fund. Besides these sums of money, another account held money that was reserved for conference construction and extensions. The Treasurer discovered that when these three funds were added up, there was already sufficient money for the Mission to purchase the property and support the missionary doctor. The Mission personnel were amazed and gave thanks to the Lord for His timely and adequate provision. God was already in our future.

THE CAMPBELLVILLE CAMP AND CONFERENCE CENTRE IN ONTARIO

During the initial days of the Mission in Canada, the Council acquired a beautiful home at 86 Woodlawn Avenue, Toronto. That house served as the Mission headquarters, a home for the staff and, for a short while, a Bible college. At that time the premises were ideal. Public transport was convenient, and because Toronto traffic was much lighter than today, workers could easily travel all over the city. In 1994 we decided to sell that Toronto property and seek a place that would be more suitable as a head office for the Mission and where we could have camps each summer.

What we would have normally considered being a "chance meeting," was, in fact, a God-appointed encounter. In a shopping mall in Oakville, I bumped into a Christian real estate agent. I mentioned to him that we were planning to sell the Faith Mission property and were on the lookout for another location. He then told me of a centre that was for sale but had not yet been advertised. Within a few weeks of that encounter, we met with the owners of the beautiful centre at Campbellville, Ontario, and were able to purchase the excellent property with the money from the sale of the Mission's Toronto home. The Lord already had this place reserved for us.

Conference and Camp Centre at Falkland B.C.

With the development of the Mission's work in B.C. and the periodic changes in staff, God led the Mission to focus on a more concentrated work in the interior of the province. The Surrey Centre, near Vancouver, had served the Mission well for years, but it was now far from most of the areas where the Mission was operating. It therefore became apparent that we needed a centre that would better meet the needs of the Mission.

The Lord led Brian Spence, the Mission's Area Director for B.C. at that time, to a suitable centre in Falkland that was for sale. At its height, this centre accommodated up to three hundred people, but it needed a lot of upgrading. Negotiations went on for over a year until the very week when the sale of the Surrey Conference Centre was completed. The final settlement allowed the Mission to proceed to purchase the Falkland Centre.

* * * * *

Brian Spence, the Mission's Area Director for B.C. when we purchased the Falkland Centre, looks back with gratitude to God for his conversion and experience with the Mission:

"Go west young man, go west." The late Hugh Jamieson thundered out these words across a packed Faith Mission Youth House Party in the Hamilton Road Methodist Church Hall, Bangor, Northern Ireland. The Youth House Party was an

Chapter 19—How God Provides

event that ran in conjunction with the annual Faith Mission Easter Convention at the seaside resort.

As a young convert, God significantly used that visit to the Convention to confirm a clear call to a life of Christian ministry. This event also stirred within me a desire to work with the Faith Mission (in Canada) after I listened to passionate reports from visiting Canadian workers.

Several years passed before the realization of that initial vision, including two years at the Faith Mission Bible College, Edinburgh. I spent another five years as a Faith Mission evangelist in Northern Ireland. My wife, Julieanne, and I began to sense that God was stirring our nest. The time we spent in Northern Ireland's Northwest District is filled with fond memories of a season of ingathering as we laboured in the Roe Valley area. However, God was calling us to a new sphere and a new mission field called Canada.

On a very wet morning in August 1993, we flew out from Glasgow Airport to arrive in a hot and humid Toronto, Ontario. Initially, we worked for several years on the Niagara Peninsula, while based in Hamilton, Ontario.

Following those years of blessing with the Mission, the Lord clearly called us into pastoral ministry in Waterford, Ontario. After several years in pastoral work, the Lord began to stir the nest again, with a clear call back to the Faith Mission. However, this time He placed a particular burden for the Mission's work in British Columbia. This move was confirmed when the General Director, John Bennett, met with us to confirm our acceptance back into the work.

John Bennett went on to inform us that he and the Mission Board were sending us to work in the interior of British Columbia. By this time our family had increased with the addition of our three children; Rebekah, Nathan, and

Aaron. It was with great excitement that we began the long journey west, trailing our U-Haul truck packed with all our earthly belongings. The almost 4000 kilometre journey to the Okanagan took eight long days.

We arrived in Vernon B.C. on May 5th, 2002. The weather was pleasant, and the scenery was delightful, but we didn't know anyone in the town, so we unloaded the U-Haul and moved into our rental home.

We lost no time in starting to visit local churches and pastors throughout the valley. As a result, we were able to organize several VBS outreach events, and amazingly, our summer schedule filled up quickly. Faith Mission workers have laboured in the Okanagan as far back as the 1950s, making the Crescent Beach Mission their base. From there, Cathie Macaulay and others travelled up into the interior to periodically engage in evangelistic outreach. These early workers lived in a trailer and traversed the area on bicycles. One area that they frequented was Falkland. I mention this because it was to this particular area that God helped us begin a new chapter of the Mission's work in B.C.'s interior.

God had clearly called us to B.C. and imparted a burden to establish a camp ministry there. We saw the value of camps during our time in Northern Ireland and Ontario. This burden for a camp in BC intensified and the hunt for a suitable property began. The journey took several years during which a local realtor took us to many properties, but none seemed to meet the requirements.

Eventually, we began to realize that what we needed was a purpose-built facility that was especially zoned for camp ministry. However, we asked ourselves, who is selling their camp site? Not very many camps were for sale in the Okanagan. At least that's what we thought.

Chapter 19—How God Provides

I often drove by the Okanagan Pentecostal Camp (PAOC) on my way to Falkland and Kamloops. Many times I thought about stopping by and taking a look at it. I dismissed the thought thinking, "What's the point; I'm sure the PAOC are not selling their fine property."

One day I received a call from a pastor in Cherryville, B.C., inviting me to preach for him while he attended a PAOC pastors' retreat. During the conversation, he informed me that the retreat was to be held at another location as the PAOC camp was for sale.

The excitement in my voice caused the pastor to make a call to confirm that what he had told me was true. The next day he called back to confirm that the Falkland PAOC Camp was indeed for sale. He also said that a certain group was already involved in serious negotiations with the PAOC Board. We soon made some inquiries and discovered that the interested group was at an advanced stage, but they were having difficulties raising the necessary funds.

The PAOC Board then entered into serious negotiations with the Faith Mission Board about the sale of the property. They wanted to know our vision and intention in purchasing the camp facilities. Once this information was communicated, the Board was satisfied with our vision to use the camp to reach the lost and minister to believers for revival.

In due course, after a price was agreed and the necessary paperwork signed, the property became Faith Mission's Falkland Centre. During the first winter, extensive renovations were carried out in preparation for our first summer camp.

Year by year, new ministries were added to the schedule with a Men of Honour Retreat, a Women of Strength Retreat, Winter Snow Camps, Marriage Retreats, Thirsting for God Conferences, and Christmas in the Valley, offering a complimentary Christmas meal along with a Gospel presentation. Several hundred people from far and near gather at these events each year.

Additional renovations have been carried out over the years ensuring a comfortable and pleasant environment for our guests. God has wonderfully provided for all of this to happen and to Him, we ascribe all the praise. Lives have been changed and transformed through the ongoing ministry of the Falkland Centre and to God, we give all the glory.

Homes for Mission Staff

During the Mission's early years, most staff had a room in the Mission's house at Woodlawn Avenue, in Toronto. For many years the property had also served as a headquarters for the Mission and a Bible School for seven years. From that house, the workers travelled to their respective locations. As time passed, it became clear that a much more effective work could be accomplished by having workers based in the areas where they could serve local churches in a more concentrated ministry. This meant that permanent accommodation had to be found in various places.

This necessity became a focus of prayer, and the Mission's Board followed God's leading in seeking to purchase suitable homes. God, in His own amazing way, provided through the generosity of His people and the sale of our own property so that suitable houses were acquired debt free. Between 1993 and 2016 the Mission was able to purchase homes in Mount Forest, Napanee, King Kirkland, Mount Hope, Milton, St. Thomas, Kamloops, Vernon, Melford and Red Deer. The properties in Kamloops, Melfort and Mount Forest have since been sold and money recycled to secure other acquisitions and help build new homes at the Falkland and Campbellville Centres. In answer to the prayers of

Chapter 19—How God Provides

God's people, the Lord provided every dollar so that the Mission workers were able to occupy each home debt free.

Vehicles and Equipment

During the last ninety years, God has supplied all kinds of provisions for His servants in many wonderful and diverse ways. Countless stories could be shared of how God provided suitable vehicles, houses, and equipment—always, just at the right time. John Bennett tells of few of these incidents:

> *Soon after the Mission acquired the Campbellville Centre, we needed a large quantity of beds. We received a quote of $3,000 from a source that would supply them. At a Mission Board meeting one evening it was agreed to order the beds as soon as finance became available. On the very next day, we received a letter from a person we did not know with a cheque for exactly $3,000. An accompanying note said that we were to use the gift to purchase something for the new centre at Campbellville. We placed our order immediately.*

* * * * *

> *The need for a change of vehicle for the work in B.C. was on the agenda of another Board Meeting. The Director was instructed to inform the staff in B.C. that they had the Mission's approval to change the vehicle as soon as they had the finances. The Director had no sooner relayed this information to the B.C. Director than he had a return call to say that within an hour they had received a cheque from a charitable foundation in Scotland that would cover the cost of the change of vehicle. The trustees of that foundation had not only met weeks earlier and agreed to send that gift, but the Mission had never received any-*

thing from that foundation previously. Furthermore, the trustees knew nothing of the need for a new vehicle in B.C. This is a testimony to the Bible promise in Isaiah 65:24: "Before they call, I will answer; and while they are yet speaking, I will hear."

* * * * *

One day John Bennett was working in the office at Campbellville when a man came by for a visit. He had never been to the centre before. After a short time of fellowship, he asked if the Mission had any needs with which he could help. John explained the Mission's policy of not making needs known except to God. The visitor said how thrilled he was with that policy.

Before leaving, the visitor went to his truck and returned with a cheque for $5,000. After he handed it over, John felt free to share with him how earlier that morning he had written cheques to pay bills and was awaiting God's provision before mailing them. The gift was sufficient to cover them all.

* * * * *

Ken and Louise Clipsham were returning on the ferry from Vancouver Island to finalize their accounts for the quarter when they met a Swiss couple on vacation. During their conversation, the Clipshams discovered that the husband and wife were Christians. Ken and Louise invited the vacationers home for a meal after which, Ken took them on a guided tour of Vancouver's popular sites. Later, they parted with prayer. After the visitors exited from the car Ken discovered that they had left three travelers cheques and a note saying that the money was for the Lord's work. Each cheque was worth a hundred dollars, totalling the exact amount that was needed to keep the end of quarter in balance.

Chapter 19—How God Provides

A man called at the Falkland Centre one day, just at the time when the Board was considering building a house for the manager. When the visitor heard about the proposed building, he volunteered to undertake the project. That saved the Mission thousands of dollars.

On another occasion, a team of workers volunteered to stucco the entire exterior of the main building at the Falkland Centre. Through the years other volunteers gave their time and talents to help maintain the Mission properties, serve meals and counsel at camps.

John Bennett surveys with gratitude all that God has done. The Psalmist reminds us that God opens His hand and satisfies the needs of His people. John added the following:

Space does not allow me to tell of the hundreds of faithful people who have given both large and small sums of money. They have given generously and sacrificially to invest in the Kingdom of God through the Faith Mission. Many times we prayed about a need in the morning and God's provision came in the mail that same day. We affirm, "This is the Lord's doing and it is marvellous in our eyes."

Lest anyone should get the wrong impression, we should not think that God gave us everything we had asked. There were times when we had to wait and repeatedly plead. There were also occasions when God did not provide. We have learned, as a former Board member put it, "God said He would supply all our needs. If He does not supply what we ask for, it is because He knew we did not need it." How true!

CHAPTER 20

Praise and Testimonies

In the Apostle Paul's first letter to Timothy, he expressed his gratitude for the ministry that had been committed to his trust. He proceeded to give testimony of what God had done for him through grace and love that was manifest in Christ Jesus. Paul burst into an overflowing doxology of praise, *"Now unto the King eternal, immortal, invisible, the only wise God, be honour and glory for ever and ever. Amen."*

Paul's note of overflowing praise could be re-echoed when the ministry of the Faith Mission (in Canada) is recalled.

Martin Quigley, Vice President of the Faith Mission (in Canada), relates his testimony:

My first encounter with the Faith Mission (in Canada) was in the summer of 1993. It was a beautiful Sunday evening down at the harbour front in Burlington, Ontario. We were conducting our weekly Sunday outreach to the local community. Following a time of prayer, some songs and a Gospel presentation using the sketch board, our small group of believers mingled with the crowd to hand out evangelistic literature and witness to individuals.

My family and I had emigrated from Dublin, Ireland to Canada the previous year. It so happened on this Sunday evening, after we had preached the Gospel, I was standing beside someone who seemed very interested in what we had been saying. As I turned to witness to this unknown person, I asked him if he was a Christian. When he assured me he was, I detected his Irish accent. I then asked what part of Ireland he came from and he told me he was from the South. He also added that he and his wife, Isabel, and their family, had emigrated from Ireland to take the position of Director of the Faith Mission (in Canada). This was the first time I met John and Isabel Bennett.

John also perceived my Irish accent, and straight away we began to talk about the Gospel and life and happenings back in Ireland. He asked me when I had become a Christian. After I had shared my testimony with him, he said, "We have prayed for you for more than eight years."

I was surprised and asked how he knew about me. John told me how they had arranged a meeting in Ballymena for Walter Burrell, a Seamen's Christian Friends' missionary who worked on the ships in Cork. Walter had asked for prayer for two Mormon missionaries he had witnessed to on his way to the meeting.

This story goes back to a day when my colleague and I, both of us Mormon missionaries in Belfast, Northern Ireland, were doing our usual house-to-house visitation. Walter, who was on his way to that meeting, felt compelled to stop when he noticed us walking on the sidewalk in a rural area outside Belfast. Walter was shocked to hear that I was from Dublin and was a recent convert from Catholicism to Mormonism. The Port missionary witnessed to us before continuing on his journey. I later learned that everywhere Walter Burrell went, he asked people to pray for the young Mormon missionary from Dublin. I returned to Dublin December 1977 after serving the Mormon Church on a two-year mission.

Chapter 20—Praise and Testimonies

A few years later after some personal struggles and much searching, I was converted to Christ. Seven years after that first encounter with the missionary, I took my family to a meeting in a small fellowship on the north side of Dublin. During the service, a man called Walter was invited to share about his great work in County Cork. We sat near the rear of the hall with our young children, but as soon as this small man stood up, I recognized him immediately. He had a very distinctive gray beard and a pronounced Irish accent. I turned to my wife, Carole, and said, "That's the guy who stopped me many years ago near Belfast when I was a Mormon missionary and told me that no Church could save me. He said that only Jesus Christ could save."

I couldn't wait until the service was over so I could meet Walter and to tell him my story. What a meeting that was! I will never forget Walter's reaction. While he hugged me, tears of joy flowed down our cheeks. Walter told me he had never stopped praying for me after he had met me on the street near Belfast.

Meeting John Bennett at the harbour in Burlington that Sunday in 1993 was the beginning of a lasting friendship with him, his wife Isabel, and the Faith Mission (in Canada). When I shared how I had met Walter Burrell and how God had answered prayer, we rejoiced together. I realize that our meeting that evening was no coincidence. I thanked John for his prayers for me all those years ago.

The story doesn't end there. When our youngest daughter, Sarah, got involved as a counsellor at the Faith Mission camp in Campbellville, she met Robert, a young man from County Monaghan, Ireland. In due time they got married and following their marriage, they went on to study at the Faith Mission Bible College in Edinburgh, Scotland. After returning to Canada, they joined the Mission and served the Lord in St. Thomas, in the southwest Ontario area for three years.

We have proved that the Lord is faithful, and also discovered that prayer is a powerful tool for the child of God.

* * * * *

Graham Ghent, a Faith Mission worker in Mount Hope, near Hamilton, Ontario, gives his testimony:

It is very humbling to reflect on how God has shown us His will through the years. When we do, any sense of self-accomplishment quickly evaporates, and we are only left with God's goodness and grace to us.

My wife, Melodie, and I were saved early in life, though it is hard to pinpoint an exact time. By God's grace, we didn't have to fall too far into the fleeting pleasures of sin to realize that the temporary happiness of this world grew very dim when compared to what God desired for us. Serving God with the InterVarsity Christian Fellowship at Brock University, gave us immense joy. It also taught us that spending our lives for God's glory was better than living for self.

During our post-secondary years, God led us to become involved for a short while in mission work in East Asia. Both of us grew in our dependency on God when we found that human effort was insufficient. We realized that our gifts and abilities meant nothing if God was not in it.

After university, the Lord called us to Ontario's Northlands where the church was very small, but there was an enormous amount of work to do. While there we experienced the Holy Spirit moving in ways we had never thought possible. We were stretched to the end of our resources, taken very high and then brought very low. After attempting secular employ-

Chapter 20—Praise and Testimonies

ment, and finding success, we knew the Lord wanted us to stay in full-time ministry.

One evening we heard the gentle, but a clear call of God to the Faith Mission. It didn't take long for the Lord to confirm His calling to us and we had no doubts that we would be moving. Unknown to us, Timothy and Emma Condy, who had served four faithful years in Southern Ontario, had been struggling with answering God's call to return to Northern Ireland, knowing that their departure would leave a gap in the Mission's work in Canada. They need not have worried. The Lord had His perfect way. We and the Condys submitted our papers to the Mission Board around the same time. Subsequently, we replaced Timothy and Emma in Southern Ontario.

Initially, moving to Southern Ontario was a struggle for our family. Nevertheless, we were very well helped by our Faith Mission colleagues and the Mission supporters in our District. Everywhere we went, we were met with encouraging words and the assurance of faithful prayers.

September, 2016, marked the completion of our first full year in that region, and the Lord gave us a fresh vision and zeal for our District. We are anxious to see the churches in this area become deeply concerned for lost souls in their communities. We long to see men and women driven to their knees by a loving concern for the salvation of their neighbours. "Yet even now, declares the Lord, return to Me with all your heart, with fasting, with weeping, and with mourning; and rend your hearts and not your garments. Return to the Lord your God, for He is gracious and merciful, slow to anger, and abounding in steadfast love; and He relents over disaster."

We need a revival of prayer in our churches that will fuel our outreach methods. Instead of just running a kids' club, we hope to see churches ache over the families in their towns, so *that people pray for God to do the work. Instead of simply running drop-in centres, we pray that believers will come together in prayer to ask for the Holy Spirit to do a soul-saving work through the drop-in-centres. May God have His perfect way in our hearts and His church.*

May the name of Jesus be praised in many mouths. All glory be to God on high.

* * * * *

Jeff Goudy, a Faith Mission worker in Red Deer, Alberta, speaks of his work:

When I was five years old, my dad worked for a farm chemical company in Toronto. He was sent to Saskatchewan to do test plots in different farmers' fields. One farmer from Melfort was a Christian, and his life made a real impact on my dad. After my father had finished testing the plots, the company moved us to Calgary.

What we didn't know at the time was that this farmer and his wife had been praying for our family every day. We lived in Calgary for three years, and during that period our family went through some tough times. My dad's alcoholic addiction caused a lot of fights. I remember one night lying on my bed and listening to the fighting downstairs. My tears flowed and fears grew as I thought of my mom and dad planning to divorce and how that would split up our family. I wondered if there really was a God and I prayed to ask Him to help us.

During this time, a Christian lawyer who lived on our block invited my mom and dad to a Bible Study. At first, they hesitated, but then decided to go. I am glad to say that both of them trusted the Lord. My dad quit drinking and moved us to Melfort. for a fresh start. We began to attend the same

Chapter 20—Praise and Testimonies

church as the farmer who had prayed for us and greatly influenced my dad earlier.

After a few years, Pastor Bill MacLeod conducted a week of evangelistic meetings at our church. I was so upset on the first night and remember thinking I would daydream all the way through the service. But as Pastor MacLeod began to speak, I sensed there was something quite different about this service. For the very first time in my life, I experienced the convicting power of the Holy Spirit. That night I knew there was a God, and that He was asking me to surrender my life to Him. At first, I said, "No!" I wasn't willing to give up my life.

While this battle was going on in my heart, I was unaware of anything else around me, but at one point I looked over, and for the very first time in my life I saw my dad crying. I was so scared and wondered, "What is going on here?"

When the pastor made the altar call, my dad went forward to accept the Lord. After that, his life was transformed. A few nights later, my mom went forward, and she too was transformed. From that time on, I knew there was a God, and I knew that I should follow Him, but I didn't do it.

When I was in high school, I wanted to be good because of my parents, and because I knew I should be. Sadly, I slowly began to compromise. Initially, it was a slow downward slide, but then it just gathered momentum, plunging me downward fast and faster. I became what is described in Proverbs 5:22: "His own iniquities shall take the wicked himself, and he shall be holden with the cords of his sins."

I became a slave to sin, Satan was a terrible master. I am glad that God still pursued me. I remember at the University of Saskatchewan, my biology professor told us that he was supposed to teach us evolution, but it wasn't true. He said there is no way we evolved from primates. He went on to show us the amazing design of a plant and the human body. He made a statement that I never forgot, "Where there is design, there has to be a Designer."

I sat there in the middle of six hundred other students fighting back the tears. The professor's little statement haunted me for years.

Later, after my younger brother and I bought a business in Calgary and Red Deer, we moved to Red Deer. By this time, I was sinking deeper and deeper into depression. All the things I thought would bring me satisfaction were becoming void and empty. My mom and dad were very concerned for me. I thank the Lord so much for praying parents. When my father asked me to read through the Bible, I told him I would and for his sake I began to read. After a while, I could hardly put the Bible down.

Also, at that time in Melfort, my mom and dad went to my old room and my brother's room every night and cried out to God to save us. Dad also fasted for weeks at a time for our souls. For two years I was under tremendous conviction of sin. John 16:8 says that the Holy Spirit would convict us "of sin; of righteousness; and of judgement."

I could not get away from this sense of guilt and sin. The worst times were in the quietness of the early morning when I woke up. It was also bad when I tried to fall asleep at night, and many nights when I did sleep, I dreamt of Hell. The dream was always the same, I would start falling deeper and deeper into darkness and blackness, and then I would start screaming for help. It was terrifying and so real to me. Sometimes I ran right off the end of the bed and crashed into the furniture or pull things off the bedroom wall in an attempt to pull myself out of hell.

These nightmares only stopped when someone turned on the light, and I realized where I was. Whoever turned on the

Chapter 20—Praise and Testimonies

light often remarked, "You look terrified. Are you okay?" I wouldn't say how I really felt, but I wasn't okay. It became so bad that I was afraid to go to sleep at night.

About this time, I asked my brother, Todd, if he would go with me to the church, five doors down the block. Although I told him it was to make mom and dad happy, I really did want to go. We knew that the congregation sang for the first half hour, so we skipped that part of the service and showed up in time to hear the preacher. We sat in the balcony, planning to slip out when the preacher finished so that no one would talk to us. The pastor was very sincere, and I enjoyed listening to him.

On one of those visits to the church a man saw that we were leaving early and stopped us at the door before we could get out. Instead of remonstrating with us, he invited us to his house for lunch. We had been eating Kraft Dinner for every meal, so we gladly agreed to his invitation. The man and his wife were so kind to us and began to invite us to various events.

One day I asked my brother, "Why is Mr. Pedersen being so kind to us? What does he want from us?"

Todd answered, "I think he just loves us."

I knew he was right and their genuine love so touched me. The couple invited us to their twenty-fifth wedding anniversary, and while we were there, we met a young man, Dale, who had just become a Christian. Dale was a former drug-debt collector and had lived a life of violence. Now, his eyes shone with the love of Christ. This new convert began to call at our home every day, and then eventually moved in. He was so full of the joy and the peace of God. Every time Dale talked to us it was about his salvation, and at times he cried with joy. God powerfully used Dale to impact my life. I so badly wanted the peace he had.

I was still reading through the Bible, and one day a few weeks after Dale moved in, I was reading Galatians 5 where it gives a listing of "the works of the flesh." I realized that I did just about everything in the list. At the end of the list, it states, "They which do such things shall not inherit the Kingdom of God." At that moment I came under such a gripping conviction that I was going to Hell and would be there soon. I didn't know what to do, so I kept reading through my tears.

Towards the end of Galatians 5, I came on verses that spoke of "The fruit of the Spirit is love, JOY, PEACE...." I stopped there, and said to God, "I don't even know what these two words mean, but I so need joy and peace. I can't take the pain and emptiness anymore."

I told the Lord I was so sorry for running away from Him and that if He took me, I would give Him my whole life. I trusted in Christ to save me and asked that He would give me this joy and peace. At that moment God just flooded me with this fruit of the Spirit. It was overwhelming. The guilt and weight of my sin were gone, and I was free.

After several minutes, I thought of my brother Todd and how he needed Jesus too. So, with tears flowing down my face, I tried to tell him that I had become a Christian. Before I could speak, Todd said that he also had just trusted the Lord Jesus as Saviour. It had happened to both of us at the same time even though we hadn't talked about it.

Many times since that day I have wondered why God would save a person who rebelled and ran away from Him. The only thing I can say is, "What amazing love and grace and mercy." As an old sailor said, "After saving a wretch like me, He'll never hear the end of it."

One year later God allowed me to meet my wife Jani. When we first met, we would spend hours talking about the

Lord together and studying His Word. We became best friends as we shared a deep love for Jesus and for lost souls. I knew that this was the woman that I wanted to share my life with and her heart of surrender to the Lord made her the perfect ministry partner. I have now had the privilege and honour of serving the Lord with her for twenty-four years. It has been such a faith walk and I thank God for her quiet, servant heart and for her faithful prayers for me and our six children as well as the many people that we have ministered to.

God has definitely knit our hearts together in the areas of prayer, revival, and evangelism. There are so many ministries that I could highlight but one that has been especially encouraging is getting small groups of Christians together to pray for personal and corporate revival. It's been amazing to see God's power at work in hearts as people get honest, confess sin, and by faith cry out to God to be filled with His Spirit. As men and women and young people get their hearts right and intercede asking God to pour out His Spirit in their communities we have seen and heard great reports. God always answers and the overflow is seen in many ways including an increased burden and excitement for evangelism.

It has been a special joy for us to see so many pastors coming out to the pastor prayer groups and to witness them going through personal revival and how that has effected so many churches. These leaders are so vital and it is truly beautiful to see them coming together in prayer and unity of heart to pray and to support one another. Most recently in the area of evangelism we have been able to spend time with many newcomers to Canada. Again, amazing how God has brought many nations to Canada so that they can meet Christians and hear the gospel. We love every area of ministry and the days and weeks are full as we run many prayer groups, disciple believers, teach, preach and evangelize. Working at camp in the summer is also a blessing and has meant so much to our children over the last ten years.

One message that is so clear in my heart is that Christians everywhere need to be surrendered to Him and filled with His Spirit. It is such a simple message and at times when I try to explain about the surrendered life and the fullness of the Holy Spirit, I feel embarrassed because it is so straight forward. Through the years I've seen the reality of this truth. And as people fully give themselves to God and ask to be filled with the Holy Spirit, God gives His fullness and it is life changing.

Jesus gave the disciples very simple instructions for His Church. He said, "That repentance and remission of sins should be preached in His name among all nations, beginning at Jerusalem" *(Luke 24:47-49). He then told them how they would be able to do this impossible task:* "Behold, I send the promise of my Father upon you: but tarry ye in the city of Jerusalem, until ye be endued with power from on high." *My prayer for Canada is that He would raise up men and women in every community who would come together and pray for His promise.*

* * * * *

Jennifer Katchikian, a former Faith Mission worker, is now a pastor's wife. Jennifer wrote the following:

My name is Jennifer Katchikian. I served in the Faith Mission (in Canada) for approximately nine years. I began my ministry in Napanee, Ontario when I was twenty years old. During this time I was involved in many churches, helping run programs and events such as kids' clubs, youth groups, Bible studies, prayer meetings, conferences, music ministry, and camps. While working with the Mission, the Lord began to burden my heart for the Province of Quebec and specifically the greater Montreal area where I grew up. I prayed and asked the Lord to provide three things: a place to live, a friend/co-worker to work alongside and something to do once we were there. Within months the Lord answered this prayer.

During one of my visits to Quebec, a church offered us a rent-free manse for our accommodation. The Lord sent Debra Perron (nee Hewitt) to work alongside me. I had only met Debra once before during a teen camp in Northern Ontario. We often reminisce about those first weeks and months learning to work together and get along with each other. The Lord brought two very different people together to become great friends and true sisters in the Lord. Years later we were maids of honour at each other's weddings.

Debra and I went to Quebec with plans to run a youth group and a kids' club in two different towns. It did not take long for other opportunities to open and soon our schedule was full. We were able to hold Bible studies in a public high school and an elementary school.

I learned many valuable lessons during those years together, the two most precious being, to wait on God and let Him lead me where He wanted.

I am very thankful for my time in the Faith Mission (in Canada). The fellowship with co-workers, praying together and serving the Lord together were very special times. The Lord used the lessons I learned during those years to train me for the future and make me the person He wanted me to be.

The Naylors, father and son, are busy in the Lord's work.

> *"Great is the LORD, and greatly to be praised, and His greatness is unsearchable. One generation shall commend Your works to another, and shall declare Your mighty acts"* (Psalm 145:3-4 ESV).

One of the great privileges we have had serving the Lord in Northern Ontario is to witness God's faithfulness extended to multiple generations, and to hear testimonies of His greatness. An excellent example of this is that of the Naylor family. God gloriously saved, called and sent first the father and then the son. Here are their testimonies of how one generation commended the works of the Lord to the next.

Dave Naylor, the father, relates his story:

> *My journey with the Mission goes back to 7:30 p.m., on October 15, 1967. At the invitation of a friend, I attended a youth group at the Salvation Army in Kirkland Lake, Ontario. On that date, our group travelled together by bus, to a little country school in Dane, to participate in a youth service; the speaker was Miss Pearl White of the Faith Mission.*
>
> *As Miss White gave a clear Gospel message, the likes of which I had never heard before; I can remember being drawn in. At the conclusion of her message, she invited those who would like to ask Christ into their hearts to be their Lord and Saviour, to come forward. I knew this was exactly what I had to do, and with two friends, I made my way to a rough wooden bench at the front of the classroom. There the three of us knelt before God to receive the Lord Jesus Christ. We didn't know how or what to pray, but the gentle-voiced Miss White invited us to pray after her, repeating her words. She assured us that if we meant what we prayed, God would hear us and answer our prayers, forgiving us of our sin and making us His children. This we did.*

Chapter 20—Praise and Testimonies

That night, at that moment, something wonderful happened to me. Oh, I didn't entirely understand it, but I well remember an indescribable joy that filled my heart. Travelling home on the bus, I had to tell my youth leaders and some of my friends, and when I got home, I couldn't wait to tell my mother. That night, as mom sat on the edge of my bed, she wept great tears of joy. I was two weeks shy of my fourteenth birthday, and for me, life had begun all over again.

I have always said, that God's timing in my salvation was perfect, It always is. Things were turbulent in our home; dad struggled with alcoholism. The years that followed my conversion weren't easy. High school was rough, but I knew that the Lord loved me and He was walking beside and before me. I found great joy and strength in His presence.

I kept in touch with Miss White over the years, and it was an incredible joy to attend the Mission's Fiftieth Anniversary and share my testimony how God had used this little lady who had such a great big heart for God. She believed that a child, a youth, could be saved and that this would be the most important decision of his life. I was that child.

As church planters and pastors for over forty years, my wife, Linda, and I have had the joy of having the Faith Mission evangelists came alongside us to help with vacation Bible schools, youth groups, kids' clubs, and camps.

One of our greatest joys was in 1999 when I received a call from John Bennett. John was anxious to see the work of the Mission expanded in Northern Ontario and wanted to know if we would be willing to sit down with him to talk and pray about these possibilities. A short while after those conversations, we were pleased to host Andrew Porter and Jonathan Bennett. and introduce them to the Kirkland Lake area. The rest is history.

> *So many stories could be told. The Mission continues to have an expanded and effective ministry in many locations throughout Northeastern Ontario, and many lives have been touched for Christ and churches have been encouraged.*
>
> *the Faith Mission (in Canada) remains a small, but dynamic evangelistic arm of the Church and we thank God for you. Congratulations on your Ninetieth Anniversary. May the Lord bless and prosper your ministry until His return.*

* * * * *

Pete Naylor, Dave Naylor's son, pastors the Riverside Community Church in Swastika, Ontario. He also recounted his testimony of the part the Faith Mission has played in his life:

> *The Faith Mission has been such a blessing in our life and ministry. In fact, I may not have come to Christ myself if it had not been for the Faith Mission, under whose ministry my father was converted and called into Christian service as a young man. I grew up hearing the story of my dad coming to Christ at a youth bonfire where Pearl White shared the Gospel.*
>
> *Many years later—while finishing high school and struggling with all the things teenagers contend with regarding life and faith—I was blessed to come under the ministry of Andrew Porter who was working with the children and youth in our community and high school.*
>
> *The Faith Mission once again was a part of my personal faith journey when Andrew became a mentor and friend. Even as I went off to University and began to minister on campus with InterVarsity Christian Fellowship, I was able to coordinate for Andrew to speak to our students. He was a great blessing to us.*

Chapter 20—Praise and Testimonies

Now, in full-time ministry, planting a church in Northeastern Ontario, we have been blessed to partner with Faith Mission workers in many ventures. First, we worked with the Porters, and now with the Hardwicks. Their prayer, practical and preaching support have been a source of abundant blessing in the lives of many ministry leaders in our region. God's faithfulness in assigning these willing servants to these hard-to-reach areas has had a lasting impact that only eternity will fully reveal.

Thank you, Faith Mission! The work you do has not gone unnoticed. God the Father has prepared rich rewards by which He will honour your humble service to Him.

* * * * *

Mike Fischhoff, the Associate Director of the MoveIn Vision Team, writes in appreciation of the Faith Mission (in Canada):

Little did I know that working at the Faith Mission's summer and winter camps during my teenage years would make such an impact on my life. It was there, working with kids and youth from low-income backgrounds in Hamilton and Toronto, that I fell in love with God's heart for orphans and widows. I learned how easy it was to share the Gospel and love people from different life situations than mine. This was something I could not have learned or experienced in our church context. It was also at those camps that God spoke to me about how I would eventually be working full-time with underprivileged youth and children.

Shortly after my time at the camp, I began working with The Scott Mission's children, youth and camp department. This was not only a call to work with the poor, but to live with underprivileged children at MoveIn in the Flemingdon community. A group was formed in that community to fight sex-trafficking which is prevalent in our neighbourhood. MoveIn Vision works in eleven cities in six different countries. Seventy-one teams work with over three hundred "MoveIners." Another arm of the MoveIn is Fight4Freedom, an anti-sex trafficking organization which began in 2012. Today they have fifty-five dedicated volunteers working to reach and rescue women from the abuse of strip clubs, massage parlours and brothels. These ministries, Fight4Freedom and MoveIn Vision, are the outcome of our early years working at the Faith Mission camps.

Chapter 21

Ladies' Spiritual Enrichment Retreat

Isabel Bennett has no doubt that the "Ladies' Spiritual Enrichment Retreat" was birthed in the heart of God. Her burden and passion were for women to "come apart and rest a while." A day or a few days away from their regular Martha-like chores and routines would allow them to sit at Jesus' feet like Mary and listen to His voice through female Bible teachers. These gatherings were designed to lead ladies into deeper truths in the Word of God without the distractions of situations and circumstances. Isabel's prayer was that they could leave the conference spiritually enriched, renewed and stronger to walk with God. It was also Isabel's desire that non-Christian ladies would be able to find and accept Jesus Christ as personal Saviour.

That vision was realized in May, 1998, when the Mission's female workers hosted the first Faith Mission Ladies' Spiritual Enrichment Retreat at the Campbellville Centre. The Centre's rural surroundings make it a perfect setting for people to get away from the hustle and bustle of daily life into a serene atmosphere of peace and quiet to spend time with God. There the ladies enjoy praying together in groups, good food at meal times, and sharing sweet fellowship while they are spiritually nourished through studying the Scriptures.

These ladies come together from different denominations, from various walks of life and include the young and not so young. They spend time sitting at Jesus' feet, unburden their hearts, share their personal experiences and then pray together and for each other. God's presence has been so real at these meetings, and many have experienced God's power and blessing.

Former Faith Mission worker Hester Rendall (nee Dougan), was the guest speaker at the first Ladies' Spiritual Enrichment Retreat. With Bible in hand, Hester impressed upon the ladies the necessity and blessing of walking by faith and not by sight. She highlighted the biblical examples of Noah, Enoch, and other Bible characters.

That first retreat was such a success and the beginning of nineteen years of special events arranged for ladies. So many Christian women manifested their hunger for the deep truths of God's Word a second spring retreat and a fall retreat became necessary. These annual Spring and Fall Retreats have become regular calendar events.

A few testimonies give evidence of how God has blessed these conferences. One lady wrote:

> *Looking into the dining area, I could not help but see how tastefully the tables were prepared. China cups and saucers were neatly placed around the spring-coloured centrepieces on each table. Colour-co-ordinated serviettes were placed alongside little gifts for each guest. The first meal for the weekend was advertised as a "Special Touches" dinner, and it lived up to its name. As I observed the beautiful room, God spoke to me: "That's what I can do with your life."*
>
> *That moment was the turning point of my life. Let me backtrack a little. While riding my motorbike on the highway, I had thoughts of turning back home instead of going to the Ladies Spiritual Enrichment Retreat weekend. I was in a self-destructive mood, but something constrained me to be there. I now know it was God who was drawing me. Before the guest*

Chapter 21—Ladies' Spiritual Enrichment Retreat

speaker spoke a word, God spoke to me when I entered that dining room.

Riding my motorcycle back home along the same highway, I was a different person. God helped me get my eyes off myself and on to Him. He showed me how beautiful my life could be with His moulding and shaping.

Another lady accepted an invitation from some friends to accompany them to the ladies' retreat. When these women shared their concern for their friend's salvation, we prayed. Imagine their delight and ours when she came to the Saviour before leaving. A work of God's grace was most evident in her life for she bore a wonderful testimony. That lady continued to attend the annual retreats and live for Jesus until God took her home after a long battle with cancer.

Janet Hoover shared her experience of the Ladies' Spiritual Enrichment Retreats:

My first experience with the Faith Mission Ladies' Retreats was in 2002 when my Mom suggested that we go for the Saturday sessions. We arrived while the ladies were having their morning prayer meeting in the main auditorium. We stood in the front hall, the women were unaware of our presence, and we were unfamiliar with the surroundings, but we listened to them praying. I was struck by the sense of God's presence in that place. The Holy Spirit prompted those prayer times, and I knew that this was something that I wanted to be a part of.

Next year Mom and I returned to the retreat and brought a friend with us for the full weekend. In subsequent years we took many more friends to the meetings. The Ladies' Spiritual Enrichment Retreat became a highlight of my year so that each year I booked early to avoid any disappointment. The presence of God was the main attraction of those weekends and this was clearly seen in God's people. God's presence was sensed as exceptional speakers spoke of God's work with honesty, passion, love and in the power of the Spirit.

We also experienced His presence in sweet fellowship with ladies from various denominations and traditions with multiple backgrounds and experiences. These women were at different stages of life but all came together with a common purpose. God's presence was known as we shared our burdens, prayed and encouraged each other in the Lord. The beauty of the Lord's presence was seen in the selfless service of the Mission ladies who worked tirelessly to offer a peaceful retreat for those who attended.

For me, the ladies' retreat was an oasis in the midst of a world that doesn't hunger and thirst for righteousness. Often in the environment of our home churches, we don't have those spaces and times where meeting with God has priority. When we take time to step away from the clatter and bustle of life and stop and listen to what God wants us to hear, life takes on new clarity, our strength is renewed and life's problems diminish in the light of His presence.

I found these annual Ladies' Spiritual Enrichment Retreats were instrumental in bringing words of help and healing during several difficult years of my life. I can still recall God using significant Scriptures and illustrations as He came close to me and I sat in His presence. It is a wonderful thing to be shaped by God's hand, and the ladies' retreats offer an opportunity for this to happen.

Returning to the conference each year continued until God called us to leave our home to serve Him at the Campbellville Camp Centre. We are now in our fourth year of service with the Faith Mission. I am now on the other side of the Ladies' Retreat—the serving side. I do miss the anticipation of coming each year and being a part of the visiting fellowship. However, I have proved God's faithfulness in all situations. When we

Chapter 21—Ladies' Spiritual Enrichment Retreat

take the time to come away and meet with God, the moments have eternal potential.

* * * * *

Francine Chaisson shares:

I had always been uncertain when it came to ladies' retreats. I know it was because I was never sure how to fit in. I always felt more comfortable around a group of guys than a whole posse of women. While most folks would say that I am an outgoing person, that was only a cover-up so that people would not get too close to me and see just how weak and vulnerable I was.

At the Ladies' Spiritual Enrichment Retreats at Campbellville Centre, I experienced real heart-to-heart friendships. I was struck immediately by the ladies having a profound hunger for digging into God's Word and wanting a deeper and closer walk with Him. Women from all walks and stages of life sat down together and hungered for more of God.

I must say that our times of prayer were the most precious times for me. No time to "sit and chat," when it came time to pray. No time to "get to know one another." I can honestly say that we got to know our God, and then we got to know each other in a more meaningful and deeper way. When you pray with a small group of people, you get to know their hearts, their sorrows, their woes and their joys.

One speaker stands out; if I could only remember her name! I suppose you might think that she could not have been that impressive if I can't even remember her name. However, I do recall her talking about marriage, and I groaned within: Oh no—not a message about married life and here I am, a single lady!

That day, I realized that I always had something to learn, from any message. She spoke about how she almost split from her husband because they each had their own idea of how to squeeze the toothpaste out of the tube. This went on until it dawned on them that it wasn't the toothpaste-squeezing that was problematic; it was two stubborn hearts refusing to be one. From that, I learned that there are so many times when I refuse to be one with my Lord, over utter foolishness.

Good food, deep fellowship, sweet surroundings, great music and good preaching from the Word, were always to be had at the ladies' retreats. I miss them dearly!

Faith Mission Men

Faith Mission Men was formed in 1965 when some men in the Niagara region of Ontario caught the vision to assist with maintenance of mission vehicles. As this laymen's organization developed, a membership was formed, local committees put in place, and men took on a more active role in outreach. Their stated purpose and program were detailed:

1. Faith Mission Men is a self-sustaining organization within the framework of the Faith Mission (in Canada) and is under the complete supervision of the Faith Mission Board.

2. Realizing the challenge that confronts us in rural evangelism, and the strength of a united outreach, we propose to harness dedicated Christian laymen, through prayer, planning, and programming, in an effort to extend Christ's Kingdom in our time.

3. At present we have three main thrusts:
    a. Rallies of witness
    b. Men's retreats
    c. Promoting the Faith Mission

Chapter 21—Ladies' Spiritual Enrichment Retreat

The Mission for Men meets monthly for prayer and planning.

For many years, these men manned a mobile trailer at local fairs where kids and adult meetings were conducted, Christian movies shown, and Bibles, tracts and Gospel literature distributed. They often visited every home in a community either with Gospel literature or an invitation to some special Faith Mission events or crusades.

For years these men visited every home in Dunnville where they had Sunday evening open-air services in the bandshell. They also organized special "work bees" to do maintenance on Mission properties. After the Campbellville Centre was purchased, a group of men volunteered to do most of the necessary renovating and upgrading.

We cannot overstate our indebtedness to these men, many of who are now with the Lord. Unfortunately, this organization no longer functions as it used to. Just as Elisha took up the mantle after Elijah's spectacular departure, so younger men with fresh vision and a heart for the lost are needed to step into the shoes of these men. Dr. Martin Lloyd Jones, preaching on the story of Elijah and Elisha, quoted Elisha's question, "Where is now the Lord God of Elijah?" He ended his sermon by answering, "He is waiting for Elishas to take up the mantle today."

Perhaps God is calling you, the reader, to be an Elisha in His service?

Prayer Retreats

The Lord Jesus spoke a parable to teach *"that men ought always to pray, and not to faint"* (Luke 18:1). I think the Saviour touched on the primary lesson of the parable in the final words of the verse—*"always to pray, and not to faint."* That was because we give up too soon and too often. We need to pray, but we also need to keep on praying; not giving up or losing heart.

Our great necessities and weaknesses teach us how much we must depend on God. He has provided the means of grace for us to take everything to Him in prayer. Furthermore, His great and precious promises assure us that God does answer prayer.

Throughout the history of the Faith Mission, there has always been an emphasis on prayer and persistent praying. The old adage is true, "Much prayer, much blessing—little prayer little blessing." Regular Prayer Retreats are organized because we need God's blessing on every part of this work.

Dale Callahan highlights the benefits of the Prayer Retreats, when men come together to seek God's blessing on their lives and the Faith Mission's ministry.

Dale wrote the following about all these seasons of prayer:

The greatest gift that God gives to us is Himself. That is what the Apostle John affirmed in 1 John 4:9: "By this the love of God was manifested in us, that God has sent His only begotten Son into the world so that we might live through Him." *The truth of the Gospel is God giving Himself for His enemies to make them His friends. As Christians, we must reject the thinking that the Gospel is only for evangelizing unbelievers. We need to be reminded daily that the Gospel is also for us.*

The Gospel of Jesus teaches that God loves and pursues the friendless. He does so to forgive sinners and become their Heavenly Father. Amazingly, God becomes their Friend.

We can begin our walk with God in the full assurance that He accepts us solely on the merits of the precious blood of Jesus Christ and His imputed righteousness. Alas, at times we take our eyes off Christ and begin to think our acceptance before God depends on us. Christians who fall into this trap often struggle with having a deep and consistent prayer life. They mistakenly think that their poor performance causes

Chapter 21—Ladies' Spiritual Enrichment Retreat

God to put out a "Do Not Disturb" sign, presuming their sin and weakness excludes them from entering God's Throne Room. The good news of the Gospel reminds us that this is not true. God always delights in His children. Our full acceptance before Him has always been and will always be because of Jesus Christ alone.

God's Word reminds and encourages us to seek Him in prayer. When He saved us He made us members of His body, the Church, and in doing so surrounded us with family "friends."

The greatest friendships I have known happened when we encouraged each other to seek God in prayer. We came before Him together, confessed our sins before God, praising Him for His greatness, thanking Him for all of His gifts, interceding for the salvation of others, crying out for His strength, and asking Him to make us more like Jesus.

A few months back I had the joy of travelling six hours to meet with a group of men for a Prayer Retreat. My first Christian friend from twenty-five years back, Jeff Goudy, invited me to join them before God's throne. For me, it was a Royal invitation I did not want to turn down.

As I stood around the campfire with thirty men, all singing God's praises before we prayed, I understood more clearly the Faith Mission's heart and why my friend Jeff, by God's grace, had focused for years on gathering men to pray.

Christian men of varying age groups and from different denominations stood around the campfire to pray for revival. It suddenly dawned on me as I looked around that the Lord Jesus' High Priestly prayer for unity among His followers was answered among us. The first answer to prayer and steps for revival had already begun.

CHAPTER 22

Kids' Clubs and Camps

The greatest investment we can make is to influence boys and girls and to introduce them to Jesus Christ. The work among kids can be demanding and exhausting, but the Lord of the Harvest asked us to pray for "labourers" and not "loafers." Christian work is not easy, not in any realm, nor did our Lord ever promise it to be. Self-denial was the pattern the Saviour set for those would follow Him. He pledged to make His followers "fishers of men." The primary calling of Faith Mission workers is to take up the cross and follow Christ. Although it does involve denial of self, it can also produce abundant blessings.

Every new generation of Faith Mission workers discovers that children's and camp work have been amongst the most fruitful ministries.

Glenn Deane, Teaching Pastor at Bracebridge Baptist Church, Ontario, enjoyed his important and strategic ministry among children and young people while working with the Faith Mission (in Canada). Follow his report:

> SCHOOL IS OUT, AND IT'S TIME FOR SUMMER HOLIDAYS!
> *School break is a perfect time for Vacation Bible School (VBS) when children are looking for something to do. Some new contacts and many churches we had helped previously, contacted*

us to help in their outreach to children. These churches had the heart for children and wanted to do something. Flyers were distributed, and news quickly spread—it's VBS time!

OUR FOCUS: *The fun of singing, memory verses, Bible stories, crafts, and games attract children. Our focus is to give them the Gospel. We hold these events across Southwestern Ontario. Some vibrant, growing churches are looking for assistance to give their regular workers a break. Some small and struggling churches are not able to run a program on their own and ask for our help. These churches are located in towns or villages that are bursting with children who need Jesus to be their Saviour and Friend.*

Sometimes the group of children starts out quite small, but by the end of the week, there is nearly always a marked increase. Of course, the best advertisement for the meetings is the children's enthusiasm in bringing their friends. Our approach to the teaching is simple, Bible-based, trusting the Holy Spirit to work in their hearts.

MAILBOX CLUB: *After the VBS finishes, many of the children have no more Christian influence until the next summer. One way we stay in touch is through the Mailbox Club. This is a Bible correspondence course offered free to all the children. Those who make a profession of faith during the VBS are also contacted this way. The contact helps maintain their enthusiasm to learn more about God's Word. The Bible lessons are written for ages from four-year-olds through to adults. It has been exciting for us to see several parents accompany their children in the studies this year. We currently have fifty-eight children and four adults enrolled.*

At the end of most lessons, the reader is invited to answer this question: "What is the most important thing you have learned in this lesson?"

Here are some of the responses we have received:

"To believe in God and Jesus because that is our salvation to Heaven."

"It is important to follow and obey God's commandments and to praise, honour and obey Him."

Other notes were written with the following comments:

"I do believe that God! Jesus loves me and wants what is best for me. I trust Him and pray for Him to guide me in the right direction."

"I do have a Bible although I don't read it every day. I want to start, but always put it off or forget. I think I obey, love, and serve God daily, at least I try to very hard."

"Thank you so much for the lessons. The children and I really enjoy them. Could you please send more?"

Highlights from VBS and Mailbox Club

One of the highlights for us this year was the testimony from a mom who wrote the following letter:

Thank you for the Mailbox Club lessons for the boys...I wanted to mention M's paper to you. As you can see on his paper, when I asked him the questions about salvation those are the answers he gave. M. had answered "Yes" to the question "Have you taken the Lord Jesus as your Saviour?"

I was not aware of a time when he had done this, but we had a good discussion about salvation and I left it with him. We finished filling out the questions sheet and he headed off to play while I worked on supper. Five minutes later he came back and said, "Mom, do you know what I did?" I said "No." M replied that he went to his room and prayed to ask Jesus to forgive him. He said he wanted to be sure that he was saved and that he told Jesus that he wanted to follow Him and not Satan anymore.

Praise God. I want to thank you for your part in this. God used not only the Mailbox Club but also VBS to touch his young heart.

Camp Ministry

Summer camp is also very fruitful. Having the children stay for a few days or a week gives us more opportunity for one-on-one contact with them, particularly to talk about spiritual matters. Two young people from our home church helped with Faith Mission camps and they shared the following:

I just like the way that you can build relationships with the kids because you are with them for a whole week and it leads to opportunities for them to see how you live and why you're different. I had the privilege of leading one boy who was in my cabin to Christ. I really enjoyed myself and it was an opportunity for growth in my own life.

I liked it. It was a really neat experience. All the girls in my cabin were Christians, so during devotions the other counsellor and I had to come up with things that they hadn't heard before. It was neat to get to spend lots of time with them. During their rest time, I could spend an hour myself reading my Bible and getting to know God better.

CHAPTER 23

On Others' Shoulders

We all stand on the shoulders of the generations that preceded us and owe them a great debt. That is certainly true of the Faith Mission (in Canada). Many of our faithful forerunners are now with the Lord, and others are retired. We highly esteem these senior fellow-workers such as Ken Clipsham, Cathie Macaulay, Ann Jamieson-Krampitz, Hester Rendall, and Nellie Buchanan, who already *"fought a good fight"* and are still making a vital contribution in prayer for the work. Their lives are a challenge and shining examples of faithfulness, perseverance, and godliness. If each were to tell their story, one book would not contain the whole accounts.

The original Faith Mission workers in Canada certainly laid a good foundation for us to continue in their footsteps. Here we provide the testimony of some who are still diligently serving God both as volunteers and full time workers.

Jim Travis's accounting and bookkeeping skills combined with his knowledge of government rules and regulations have been, and continue to this day, to be one of the great blessings God has given to the Faith Mission (in Canada). There is no doubt he has been God's man who was sent at God's appointed time. Here he shares how he became involved volunteering with the Faith Mission:

My wife Jan and I grew up attending the same church and Sunday school in St. Catharines, Ontario. Even so, we didn't acknowledge the existence of each other until we were almost twenty years old. Sadly, by that time our church had become very liberal, and we never heard of our need for personal salvation.

Fortunately for me, I spent a good deal of time as a young man with my father's parents at their home in Eden, Ontario. I was expected to attend every service at their church as well as Sunday school and any events for children. While there I heard the Gospel and was reminded about my need of Christ and salvation. Furthermore, my grandparents spoke to me about the Lord, as did an aunt. I still have a copy of Hurlbut's Story of the Bible *that she gave me when I was a young boy. I read it through many times. Even so, at that time, I didn't become a Christian.*

In my second year in high school, I decided to attend noon-hour meetings of the Inter-School Christian Fellowship. When the Gospel was clearly presented, I suddenly became very aware that I needed to be saved. It was then I received Jesus as my personal Saviour. I am sure that what my grandparents and aunt had shared with me, and what I heard at the Eden Church played a large part in my conversion to Christ on that day.

Faith Mission Contact

I first heard mention of the Faith Mission in the mid-1970s, when the pastor of our church in Oakville testified that the Faith Mission workers were preaching in Burlington, where his father was a pastor. As a lad under their ministry, he had accepted Jesus Christ as Saviour. However, we did not know much about the Faith Mission until John and Isabel Bennett,

Chapter 23—On Others' Shoulders

the newly appointed as Director of the Faith Mission (in Canada), and their boys began to attend our church in 1992.

We were invited to prayer meetings at their home, where we learned to appreciate and pray for the work of the Faith Mission. We also saw John and Isabel's personal commitment and dedication and that of the other workers to Christ and the Mission. What struck us most was that the Faith Mission did not engage in fund-raising events or soliciting for money. The workers lived by the "faith principle," and we saw how God honoured that faith.

When I was in my late fifties, my wife, Jan, and I began to discuss and pray about what I would do in my retirement years. Having enjoyed my work as a chartered accountant, we wondered if, when that time came, I might be able to become a volunteer for some worthwhile organization, where I could put my accounting experience to good use. We had not mentioned this to others, nor had the Faith Mission crossed our minds.

Shortly afterward, following a prayer meeting at their home, John Bennett asked if he could speak with me. In what the world would consider "just a coincidence," he explained that the Faith Mission's Treasurer, Ken Clipsham, was hoping to retire soon. He proceeded to ask if I would consider taking on the Faith Mission as a bookkeeping client. He explained that this would help them with their immediate needs until they could find a replacement for Ken.

There was no need for me to perform an audit of the Mission's financial statements as a firm of Chartered Accountants well versed in the audits of charities was engaged for that service. As Jan and I talked it over, we realized that not only had God answered our prayers as to what I would do in retirement, but He had done so much earlier than we had *expected. We agreed that I would not take on the Mission as a client, but rather do the work as a volunteer.*

On October 1, 1996, I became the Mission's bookkeeper and joined the ranks with many who assist in the Faith Mission's work. Initially, I continued in my day job as a public accountant until I retired six years later. I was then able to give more time to the Mission's needs, which continued to grow.

It has been a privilege for me to be a volunteer for the Mission and to see first hand the work that it does. I hope my efforts will help reduce the time workers need to spend on "pencil pushing," and give them more time for the ministries to which they are called.

CHAPTER 24

April's Hope

As a young girl, April Hardwick was greatly impressed with the teachings of the Second Coming of Jesus Christ and the events surrounding that event. She could not have realized then that the greater part of her life would be changed because of Christ's first coming into the world to save sinners and then be motivated to serve Him because this same Lord Jesus is coming again.

April Hardwick tells her story:

Although my earliest memories of church are positive, they were also very shallow. I loved attending Sunday school and participating in various crafts. I had an awareness of God, but was never convicted of my sin or understood the message of salvation. At high school, I led the youth group, but in reality, this was more of a social club for teens. Some friends invited me to a midweek Bible study on various occasions, but I felt that I had got enough of God in the youth room on Sunday mornings. Although I was fascinated to learn about the end times and to think how wonderful it would be to be caught away suddenly at Christ's Second Coming, I was oblivious to the fact that I had no real relationship with Him.

One Wednesday I found myself with nothing to do, and so I decided to go to the Bible study that I had repeatedly been invited to attend. As I sat there and listened to friends discuss the Scripture and talk about God, I realized they knew Him in a way I certainly did not. Soon after that, I turned my life over to the Lord and made the decision to enter full-time ministry, not knowing what shape that would take.

I met Mark during my second year of Bible college, and we were married the year we graduated. Ministry life was never boring with the Lord taking Mark from being a youth pastor to become a full-time senior pastor of a church in Lachute, Quebec, all within our first two years of marriage. During that time we had also welcomed our firstborn child. We served God in Quebec for ten years, and our family was blessed with another four babies.

Life in pastoral ministry was very busy. I was serving in various ladies' ministries, children's ministry and helping out in other areas where I could. Those years were not without their ups and downs, but we saw the Lord's miraculous provision in our lives in many ways. I learned what it meant to wholly rely on the Lord for our needs.

When I was pregnant with our fifth child, the Lord led us into contact with the work of the Faith Mission. I wasn't able to lead our VBS program because it was scheduled for the same week in which our baby was due. Faith Mission workers Jennifer Moldovan and Debra Hewitt stepped in to help, and soon they became our firm friends.

Over the next two years we got to know the work of the Mission better, and in 2011 we began to sense God's call on our lives to join the Faith Mission. Although I was confident the Lord was leading us and fully trusted that the Mission Board and Mark had prayed about us moving to Kirkland

Chapter 24—April's Hope

Lake in Northeastern Ontario, I was apprehensive and fearful in my heart. Once again, I had to lean on God to find strength to follow Him.

On arrival in the north, my fears were soon put to rest. We were immediately welcomed into a community that lives out the love of Christ in very practical ways. I've often said that the people here more than make up for the cold weather. We have been in Northern Ontario for almost five years and through that time have had our share of trials, both in work and in our personal lives. God continues faithful and has proved over and over again that He is sufficient.

During the past five years, God has taken me places I'd never thought I'd be and taught me so much through the journey. After losing a baby in the second trimester in 2013, I learned again that in my own strength, life would be impossible, but God has provided His strength as we surrender to Him. Mark and I have since welcomed another little girl to our family. That pregnancy was full of trips to medical specialists as they expected our little daughter to be affected by an antibody in my blood. By the end of the pregnancy, our doctors in Toronto were both confused and thrilled to be able to discharge us for the baby to be delivered back home in Kirkland Lake.

We were able to testify many times how many people were praying for our little one. After a brief scare in the middle of the week in which the baby was born, she continued to do extremely well and was soon completely discharged from further testing. Through my pregnancy and the first few months of her life, God proved again that He is faithful. I saw His grace and patience when I was struggling to trust that His will was perfect. At times my heart was so heavy, I didn't know what to pray, but I learned again that He is enough.

Throughout all of these experiences, I've continued to build friendships. These ladies have walked alongside me, and we have had an opportunity to glimpse what God is doing in our families and my life. This had led to some amazing conversations, and God has opened the door for me to speak into the lives of ladies I might never have met. I've also been blessed with a community of Christian women who authentically share with each other and encourage each other to a deeper walk with the Lord. I've realized the importance of intentionally building into these relationships.

My eternal hope is in Christ, and my desire is to know Him, to be like Him and be all that He wants me to be (Philippians 3:12-14). As I look to the future of the Mission's work in Northern Ontario, it is my prayer that the Lord would send genuine revival to His people.

CHAPTER 25

Table Talk

Much of our Saviour's ministry was conducted at meal tables. It is amazing that He nearly always transformed the dining room into a classroom by teaching the gathered around the table about the Kingdom of God. Andrew Porter's life was touched and influenced by God because of a meeting in a dining room.

Andrew Porter is best at telling his story:

My relationship with Canada began at the Faith Mission's Easter Convention in the seaside resort of Bangor, Northern Ireland. Even though I was born and raised in Northern Ireland, I didn't attend the Faith Mission camps or events. When I sensed God's call to go to Bible college, the Faith Mission attracted me. After enquiring about this, I was asked to attend the Bangor Convention for an interview with some of the Faith Mission staff. After that interview, I was invited to stick around for the rest of the conference to find out more about the Mission.

During a mealtime, I picked up my lunch and sat next to a man who was deep in conversation with a friend across from him at the table. I had never met either man, but both welcomed me and brought me into their conversation. As I tried to catch up on what they had been talking about, it became apparent that the man next to me was describing an evangelistic ministry in a different culture. He spoke about the challenge of resistance to the Gospel in various cultures. I was intrigued to find out where he was describing, so during a pause in the conversation, I asked where he was working. "Canada," he replied.

At one point in the conversation, the friend nearest to me asked the other man, "Would you come to help us?" At this, the friend replied that he had no intention of going but, pointing to me, declared, "He'll go with you."

Soon after the conversation ended, the two men parted company, but I spent the rest of the day with the man from Canada. His name was Roy Dreaning. Roy and his wife, Lorna, were living and working in Mount Forest, Ontario. As we attended the various Convention meetings, he talked more about the work in Canada. By the end of the day, we had made provisional plans for me to visit Canada for the summer to help with the ministry there. That was the summer of 1997.

What an amazing summer it was. Even before I landed on Canadian soil, the differences were obvious. Canada was huge. We flew over mountains, enormous expanses of forest and huge lakes. From the plane, the roads and highways were so straight and seemed to never end. On the plane's final approach, I noticed many homes with sparkling turquoise-blue swimming pools in their backyards. I thought, What have I got myself into?

I enjoyed everything about that summer. The people were so friendly, the weather was pleasant and the scenery beautiful. We did some VBSs and took part in church services every Sunday. The summer was not without its challenges. However, God gave us many opportunities to present the Gospel and blessed us with some success.

Chapter 25—Table Talk

I returned to the United Kingdom in the fall to begin two years at the Faith Mission Bible College. During those two years, I kept in touch with the Mission staff in Canada, and my burden for the work grew.

In June 2000 I immigrated to Canada, and by December, Jonathan Bennett and myself moved to Kirkland Lake in Northern Ontario, a very remote area. There are small pockets of farmland, here and there, but the countryside is largely comprised of forests, rocks, and lakes. Most of the population live in small towns and villages, and the main industries are logging and mining.

We were not the first Faith Mission workers to serve in that area. Years earlier, some Mission colleagues were involved in kids' ministries in homes, one-room schools, and churches. As we connected with churches in the area, some adults testified that they first heard the Gospel from those Faith Mission workers and had accepted the Lord as Saviour. They spoke fondly of the impact the Mission's workers made on them.

Jonathan and I came alongside these churches to help with their Gospel outreach. Although the communities were small, there were still lots of people who did not attend church and had never heard the Gospel. Most congregations in local churches were mainly comprised of seniors; however, they had a true burden to reach out to young people. We were able to help focus on these youth groups. Each night we had games and fun activities, snacks, and food followed by Bible time and prayer. In that way, we were able to present the basics of the Gospel to them for they had no Bible knowledge or Gospel background.

After some time Jonathan got married and moved to Faith Mission ministry in the Napanee region. Melissa and I were married almost two years after I arrived in the region, and we continued with the Northern work. For twelve years

> *we enjoyed working alongside those local churches. While I had opportunities to preach, Melissa was involved in ministry with ladies, children, and youth. We were also able to start a summer camp for these kids.*
>
> *Those were very hard years, but we learned a lot. Most of all, we learned to trust God and expect Him to work in hearts and lives. During our time there we rejoiced to see people accept Christ as Saviour, grow in their faith, and become involved with their churches. Besides preaching week by week in local churches during their pulpit vacancies, we also spent time speaking and praying with church leaders about their ministry.*
>
> *Throughout our years of ministry, we proved Psalm 126:6 to be true:* "He who goes out weeping, bearing the seed for sowing, shall come home with shouts of joy, bringing his sheaves with him."

* * * * *

Life took another favourable turn for Andrew when he met and married Melissa. These two lives were united to work for Christ in Northern Ontario.

Melissa Porter gives details of her experience in the work of the Faith Mission:

> *After Andrew and I had married in March of 2002, I joined him in the Faith Mission work in Northern Ontario. Andrew had already been working for a year and a half. The local economy at that time wasn't good. The town had been built around the gold mine after the precious metal was first discovered in Kirkland Lake early in the twentieth century. When local authorities began to tear down old houses, they discovered that these primitive structures had been built on dynamite boxes and old newspapers were used for insulation.*

Chapter 25—Table Talk

Kirkland Lake had grown too quickly, and since there was no town planning at that time, houses were built randomly wherever land was available. The lack of planning resulted in a hodgepodge of streets going in every different direction.

With the discovery of gold, there were plenty of jobs, and this attracted thousands of hopeful prospectors and workers to the area. At its peak, the population reached around 70,000. When the value of gold dropped, it became cheaper to mine in other parts of the world, with the result that Kirkland Lake declined significantly. When we arrived in 2002, the population had been reduced to around 10,000 and property was extremely cheap.

No more than a hundred local people attended any Protestant church on Sundays, and most of those were senior citizens. Andrew had been renting a small apartment, but when plans were made for our wedding, he rented a small house. The owners had been trying to sell the house as they had moved to another town. The house continued to be for sale while we were living in it.

We arrived back from our honeymoon, excited and eager to begin working together. With the massive decline in local church attendance, there were abundant opportunities to work with children and youth. Andrew also had many opportunities to preach during pulpit vacancies.

In time, Andrew found a small house for us in the village of King Kirkland, which consisted of about a hundred homes. We unpacked our boxes and set up our first home. We were overjoyed when some visitors stopped by to welcome us to the area.

Three weeks after moving in, we awoke one morning to find our house unusually cold. Although it was March, some snowdrifts had not yet completely melted. The landlords had filled the oil tank just before we moved in, so it seemed strange that the furnace wasn't working. Andrew had a preaching engagement about three hours away that day, so there wasn't much time to figure out the problem. After he preached, we had lunch and drove leisurely back home. When we arrived, we discovered that the house was even colder than when we had left. Andrew checked the oil tank, and it was empty, which seemed unusual.

We determined to find out the cause of the problem next morning. After calling the landlords to have the oil tank filled, it was discovered that ice had fallen off the roof onto the fuel line and broken it. Consequently, the oil had spilled and seeped into the ground. The spillage was an environmental problem as the local homes drew their water from individual wells.

For the next three weeks, because we had no central heating in the house, we had to use space heaters. We watched trucks and workers drilling and digging all around the house, investigating where all our oil had gone.

On Wednesday afternoon, three weeks later, we received a call to notify us that the oil had leaked into the soil below the house, and because of the environmental hazard, the house had to be demolished for them to decontaminate the soil.

A bulldozer was scheduled to come on Friday, two days later. We immediately began to look for another place to stay. There was nothing available to rent, but we believed God would provide, so we started to pack up our belongings. Andrew had a previous engagement on Thursday, so I packed our belongings that day. The phone began to ring with neighbours offering to help us move the following day.

On Friday morning, we had all our boxes packed; friends arrived to help move our stuff, but we had nowhere to go. Andrew and I went downstairs to pray. Andrew had peace and confidence that God knew what we needed and He

Chapter 25—Table Talk

would provide. I wasn't so sure. We prayed, and since we didn't have a place to go, we told everybody to go home.

The bulldozer still hadn't arrived, so we felt we had a little more time. By Friday at supper, we figured we had some respite as the workers might not come over the weekend. Andrew had to preach on Sunday, so while he spent Saturday preparing for his message, I was bored with nothing to do since everything was packed. We only had a few disposable dishes and cutlery.

On Saturday night we received a phone call. A neighbour was going for a walk and noticed an empty house nearby. Upon inquiry, we discovered that the tenants had just left. After a few phone calls, we arranged to meet the owners on Monday morning.

As soon as we walked into that house, we could see that it was well built. We immediately realized that God had not only provided a place for us to live, but He had also provided abundantly more than we could ask or imagine. It was in a fantastic location, with lots of space for mission activities and guests. We moved in almost immediately, and a few years later the Mission purchased the house.

An eight-year-old boy came to our summer Daily Vacation Bible School each day in the village community centre. We had between five to eight kids each day who were well behaved and listened well. To help them learn Bible verses, we had a competition with an incentive of a prize at the end of the week.

Colton, an eight-year-old boy, was unable to come on Friday, so he stopped by our house for his prize. As he was leaving, he asked, "Will there be church again next year?" I was blown away by the thought that this V.B.S. was the only church this child had ever known.

When we were expecting our second child, Andrew was convinced that if she were a girl, we should name her Keziah. I was uncertain as it was an uncommon name. I had begun to befriend my neighbour and I prayed that if we had a daughter and named her Keziah, that God would use the name in my neighbour's life. On the afternoon that our daughter Keziah was born, my neighbour phoned me at the hospital. Hearing this biblical name, this nominally Catholic lady decided to open up her dusty Bible and search for the name. When she could not find it she Googled it on her computer and finally found it in the book of Job. After looking for Job in the Bible's table of contents, she began to read the whole book from the beginning. She went on to discuss with her husband the many things she did not understand from her reading.

When I returned home from the hospital, my neighbour told me what she had done and mentioned that there was so much she didn't understand. From that conversation, we started a weekly Bible study with another neighbour. Six months later I invited them to the Faith Mission Ladies' Retreat, six hours away from where we lived. On the Saturday night of that weekend, my neighbour gave her life to the Lord.

On Sunday morning, during a testimony time, my friend stood up and told how she had given her life to the Lord. She said, "Nine months ago a baby girl was born named Keziah...."

We were able to use the Village Community Centre free of charge for a weekly kids' club and youth group. Some children came because they were invited while others also came because they were curious or had nothing else to do. We did a series of stories through the "Life of Christ" leading up to Easter. None of the six children who attended had any church background nor did their parents or grandparents attend any church. The children always listened intently while we shared

Chapter 25—Table Talk

the Bible stories about Jesus healing the sick, walking on water and teaching the crowds.

At Easter, I began to tell the story of Christ and His suffering and death. One little girl, was so taken aback that she cried out with tears in her eyes, "HE DIES?" Our hearts were heavy with the realization that this little girl knew nothing of Christ's sacrifice, but we were also overjoyed when we told her that the story didn't end with His death. We went on to teach that although Christ died, He was no longer dead—JESUS IS ALIVE.

A couple of years later, a few families had moved away, and the decision was made to host the kids' club in our home. We sent out the regular flyers and newspaper advertisements, but only two boys came. Week after week, no matter how we bribed them, they didn't bring any friends with them. Although the two boys listened well and loved coming to our home, it was discouraging, and I felt that it wasn't worth the time. I was rebuked when God clearly spoke to me, reminding me that it was *worthwhile to invest in these two boys.*

After running the club in our home for eight months, we found out from other neighbourhood kids that the two boys had told all the other children that they were not allowed to come to the club. Those two kids wanted it all to themselves. However, years later, those same two boys shared with us how much they learned that year at our home.

Kids!

CHAPTER 26

Ready for Anything

So much of the Scriptures is taken up with horticultural and agricultural scenes and language. The Lord Jesus drew many of His teaching parables from the Galilean countryside when He spoke of seed, sowing, reaping, sheep and lambs. Kevin Evans was no stranger to life down on his family farm. It was there he learned many lessons that would help him and his wife, Janice, when God called them into the work of the Faith Mission.

Kevin and Janice Evans articulate how God worked in their lives and chose to work through them to bless others:

> I, Janice, was raised in a Christian home where my parents, siblings, and extended family modeled Christ-like living. At the age of four, with the help of my mom, I prayed and asked Jesus to forgive my sin, of which I was very aware. Daily family devotions, Sunday School, Kids Klub led by my mom, and Summer Bible Camp, all helped me grow in my faith.
>
> I, Kevin, was raised in a wonderful Christian home where my parents, five older siblings, and grandparents loved and served the Lord. I was nine years old when I repented of my sin and gave my life to the Lord. God saved me and set my feet on a good path. I didn't experience the horrors that so many in our world grow up with: divorce, foster parents, drug, and alcohol

abuse, a life of habitual sin. God spared me from so much. I was raised on our family farm in Saskatchewan; a great place for a kid to grow up. I always knew I'd be a farmer. I met the love of my life at summer Bible Camp when we were sixteen years old, and we married three years later.

For twenty years, working on the family farm, God used us in leading youth, children's ministries, and home discipleship Bible Studies. But as the farm became more and more diversified to stay afloat, our time for ministry was squeezed out. It was then that God called us to leave the family farm to be available to go anywhere He called. Two years later He directed us to a church plant in Vernon, B.C. where we led children's and family ministries. That was the toughest thing we and our five children, ages eight through sixteen years old, have ever done. However, we really learned to trust the God we loved and served. He taught us so much that prepared us for things ahead. To make ends meet, Kevin did home renovation work on the side.

In 2007, after Kevin had been in B.C. for two years, the Faith Mission purchased the old Pentecostal camp near Falkland and he was hired to renovate the washrooms. That was our very first introduction to the Faith Mission, and we became very interested in the work. During that first summer of camp, Janice taught the Bible lessons in Chapel and later spoke at the first B.C. Ladies' Retreat in October. As the church in which we were serving merged with another church, in the overlap of staff, we believed we should step back. We resigned, and applied to join the Faith Mission November, 2007.

In August 2008, we were relocated to Kamloops, B.C., where God opened many doors for ministry. Within the first few months, we began teaching Bible clubs for kids in four elementary schools in and around Kamloops. Very soon we were leading five clubs a week, teaching Bible stories to chil-

Chapter 26—Ready for Anything

dren who had never heard. Kevin got involved in prison ministry as well as working with men with addictions. Together we began to lead Marriage Enrichment Retreats, which have been a real passion for us. These are designed to help build marriages based on biblical principles. We also taught parenting classes at the Pregnancy Care Centre, besides our involvement at the camp and retreats.

Our favourite story of a life transformed by the power of the blood is that of Cam, in prison for manslaughter. He was a rough, tough guy, whose life was messed up from money and alcohol. In prison, he began to read the Bible and was gloriously saved. He started studying the Bible with fellow inmates, and God worked mightily in and through him. Kevin met with Cam each week, encouraging and challenging him from the Word of God. When he got out of prison early, Kevin was there to pick him up and bring him to the camp. Five months later he was enrolled in a Bible college where God continued to transform his life. Today Cam is an entirely different person, a testimony of God's grace, love, and power. To God be the glory!

We enjoyed four wonderful years of ministry in Kamloops. Then, one by one, Christians in the different communities where we led Kids Klubs told us they didn't need us anymore. They were ready to take over the ministries there. We were thrilled, but wondered what God was going to ask us to do next. That's when the Faith Mission Board moved us to manage the Falkland Camp Centre. We knew that Kevin, with his experience of fixing anything on the farm, would be a perfect fit. But Janice's heartbeat had been children's ministries for more than twenty-five years. However, God very quickly equipped her for the role of cook and hostess, and has given great joy in the ministry of "preparing the place where people come to meet with God."

God continues to teach us much about trusting Him, serving others with grace and joy, and depending wholly on Him. We have had many fantastic opportunities to pour into the lives of young helpers at camp, praying for them, and discipling them. Our Marriage Enrichment Retreats twice a year are still a highlight for us, as we humbly share God's work in our lives, and watch Him transform many marriages for His glory.

Coming from life on a farm where you just worked harder if you needed something, it has been a growing experience for us, learning to trust God for everything we need.

When we were called to move to the Falkland Camp Centre, we found that the old double-wide trailer there had suffered so much damage from a very wet spring that it was condemned. Only a few days before going, an elderly couple from our home church in Kamloops donated a fifth wheel trailer to the camp, and that became our home for many months. God had provided before we knew the need.

As we looked at options for purchasing a new mobile home, a retired building contractor whom we had never met showed up one day, offering to build us a house. What a blessing Hank and Viola Remple have been to us. They built a beautiful home for us at the camp, living on site for months until it was completed. Other tradespeople came on board, donating their time and expertise to help with wiring, plumbing, painting, landscaping, and much more. Viola has also helped in the camp kitchen for many, many weeks.

We praise God for a retired electrician friend who has used his skill to repair many issues throughout the camp property. When the gym roof needed to be replaced, God provided both the funds and a great team who did a fabulous job at a substantially reduced cost. A team from our home church in

CHAPTER 27

On the Move

Jennifer Armitage was used to changing from one location to another from her early childhood. Although she was born in England and raised in Scotland, she arrived in Canada before she was a teenager. More importantly, it was in Scotland that she trusted Christ as Saviour at a Faith Mission Camp. That early association with the Faith Mission continued when she arrived for a new life in Canada, her new world.

Jennifer Armitage is best at telling her story:

I was born in Manchester, England, and was raised by parents who, although they were believers, had lapsed and walked away from God. Because my Mom knew there was a better way to live, she sent me to Sunday school from an early age. When I was eight years old, our family moved from England to Scotland. Amazingly, when my Mom was preparing our home in Scotland and Dad was moving things from England, both of them came back to the Lord.

From that time onwards, church became an important event for the whole family. My parents had friends who mentored them, and we spent time at their house. Soon they became involved with a church and began to help in the Kids' Club that I attended. It's difficult to say all that was hap-

...able to see in my parents' lives ...pening at that time, ... just Sunday church services. For that God was ...and personal.
them, God ...time my dad, who was a trained chef, began to work... Above... Faith Mission Bible College in Edinburgh. The ...ion organized summer camps for children, and when I was ten years old, my parents sent me to one of these camps. Although I was so young, I didn't know that this camp would play such a significant part in my life. I'm not sure how much of the Bible stories I took in, but God must have been working in my heart. One night while discussing Heaven and Hell with our counsellors, I realized that without Jesus as my Saviour I would be separated from God in Hell for all eternity.

I had never heard of the Holy Spirit or that He was a real person who speaks and strives with us. I do know that a voice spoke to my heart saying, "Jennifer, if you were to die tonight, you would go to Hell." Deep down I knew this was true. I remember asking a counsellor to pray with me that night. I asked the Lord Jesus to save me from my sin.

A year after my conversion, our family moved to Canada. Because of our previous connection with the Faith Mission, my dad went to a Faith Mission meeting where he met up again with John and Isabel Bennett who were now leading the Mission's work in Canada.

When I became a teenager, I got involved in the Faith Mission summer camps and their VBS work. During that time that God began to speak to me about being a missionary even though I had no idea what that would entail. Consequently, I ended up studying for two years at the Faith Mission Bible College in Edinburgh, Scotland. I then spent another two years with the Mission in various parts of England, Scotland, Northern Ireland and Southern Ireland. Following that,

Chapter 27—On the Move

I began to question whether I should be returning to Canada or not. The question was settled in 2005 when I moved back to work with the Faith Mission (in Canada).

The Mission Board sent me to Eastern Ontario. We lived in Napanee and worked in the surrounding area for the next eight years. Our ministry was wide-ranging, taking in kids' work, youth work, and adult ministry alongside local churches. After almost twelve years working with the Faith Mission (in Canada), I am currently working in the Mission's office. I still occasionally teach at camp or engage in children's and adult ministries.

I have learned to be ready for whatever or wherever the Lord asks.

Chapter 28

Christ Alone

"By grace alone, through faith alone, in Christ alone" was the hallmark statement of the great Protestant Reformation. Although good works do not save us, we have been saved to be God's handiwork, *"created in Christ unto good works"* (Ephesians 2:10). God not only has His plan, but the Scriptures also teach that He *"works in you both to will and to do of His good pleasure"* (Philippians 2:13).

Robin and Debra Perron can trace God's gracious and providential hand, saving them, guiding, and bringing them together to serve Him.

Robin Perron testifies of God's amazing grace and providential guidance to work with the Faith Mission:

I grew up in a devout Catholic home and was raised with many good values. Some of the fondest childhood memories involve going to church with my family. However, my faith never really made an impact on how I lived. I was extremely confused about the Catholic religion, about Jesus and how it all fitted together. I grew up knowing Jesus died for my sins and I even believed it, but it never really made much sense to me or why it should matter.

As I grew older, I realized I was a sinner. I became a heavy drinker and loved partying. I wanted to be popular and have people to like me. Even though I was considered a nice guy on a worldly standard, I began to have profound conviction about my sin. This conviction followed me wherever I went, and it didn't matter what I did to try to get rid of it. Everyone around me was oblivious to what I was experiencing, but I couldn't deny what was going on inside of me. I was confronted with my many sins, and I had no idea what to do or where to turn. I felt like I was shackled in a dungeon with my sin weighing me down. I didn't talk about it with anyone. It was a secret burden I was bearing, and this went on for years.

What I didn't know was that God had already chosen me in Christ, even long before He created the heavens and the earth (Ephesians 1:4-5), and He wasn't going to let me slip through His fingers. During the years that followed, I tried to accomplish many things in hopes that they would fulfill me. I obtained a post-secondary education, worked my way up the ranks in a field-related career and bought the house of my dreams. However, all those things failed to give me satisfaction or fulfillment.

I believed in God but had no idea who He was. I did all the Catholic sacraments and performed other works such as praying to the saints and confessing my sins to a priest, but the deep chasm in my soul remained. I thought God to be cruel for not taking away my conviction of sin and sense of guilt. Drinking liquor got increasingly worse, and I started to become bitter toward the people I loved because I didn't know how to deal with the darkness inside of me. It got to the point to where the people who cared about me were afraid I was becoming an alcoholic.

I eventually returned to university at the age of twenty-six after a failed attempt following high school. Those four college years changed my life forever! Because my program had

Chapter 28—Christ Alone

many science and geology courses, my mind was filled with atheistic ideas and concepts. This caused me to start questioning the existence of God. Part of me wanted to believe there was no God in hopes that the feelings of shame and guilt would go away. The more I tried to disprove the reality of God by using the new concepts and ideas I was being taught, the more I studied them. I eventually came to realize that more faith was required to believe in those theories than was required to believe in God.

It was around this time that the Lord placed one of His faithful servants, Pete Naylor, into my life. I didn't know this at the time, but God had prompted him to present the Gospel of Jesus Christ to me and invest time in me. I'll never forget the first time he told me that Jesus had already paid the penalty for my sins and that His redeeming work was a gift that I simply had to receive and embrace.

Having experienced a works-based religion all my life without ever receiving fulfillment or inward peace, I accepted Christ's amazing gift of grace, love, kindness and mercy. I clearly understood that Jesus was the only provision for my salvation. It was exactly for this that I had been longing. I now had, and still have, a genuine peace and joy in my heart knowing that the shed blood of the Lamb of God who took away the sin of the world has covered my sins. Praise the Lord! For the first time in my life I was fulfilled spiritually, and my spiritual thirst had been quenched. My search had ended because I had found the most precious treasure that could ever be found.

Since committing my life to Jesus Christ, I have had a continual desire to become more and more like Him and to serve Him faithfully. I wanted to invest fully in things that had eternal significance and to devote myself to being part of God's plans and purposes for my life. Through a series of events and by His Word, the Lord eventually called me to serve Him full-time. When He did, however, He made it very clear that I should wait. This period of waiting was tough since I was ready to venture out into His service.

Over a year after God called me into full-time service, he brought Debra Hewitt, a Faith Mission worker, into my path. Her love for the Lord and her passionate desire to serve Him and proclaim the Gospel to children and teenagers greatly intrigued me. As I learned more about her ministry in Quebec and the heart the Faith Mission had to help and support local churches, I began to see the Lord's plan for my life unfolding before me.

Debra and I eventually married in 2014, and we have been serving the Lord together with the Faith Mission since then. What a blessing to have the opportunity to serve God full-time with my spouse and to labour in a ministry that is so faithfully dedicated to the Lord. Not only did the Lord fulfill my desire for marriage, but He also fulfilled my desire to be on a mission field where I can reach French Catholics who are under the bondage of works as I once was, rather than knowing the freedom of God's grace. He really does give us immeasurably more than we could ever ask for or imagine.

Many years following my conversion, I discovered that the father of my friend Pete Naylor, who led me to the Lord, was also saved at a Faith Mission Youth Night in Kenogami, Ontario when he was fifteen. God is so good.

* * * * *

Debra Perron also shares her personal testimony of how the Lord saved her and brought her into the ranks of the Faith Mission to work alongside her husband:

Chapter 28—Christ Alone

I was born and raised in rural Northeastern Ontario where I attended church from a young age. I always remember having faith and loving to learn more about Jesus from the Bible. When I was seven years old, I attended a VBS at my church that was organized by the Faith Mission. Hester Dougan (now Rendall) was teaching God's Word, and as she was speaking, the Lord spoke to my heart. I felt like I truly understood for the first time that my sin separated me from Christ, and I recognized my personal need for a Saviour. I remember approaching Hester after the meeting and praying to the Lord for forgiveness. I believe that on that day I was saved and my journey of following Christ began.

As I grew up, I had a love for God's Word and God kept me close to Him. My teenage years were spent serving in my local church and helping to run my church's youth group. I am so thankful for the people who poured themselves into my life, loving and teaching me about the Lord. I am now seeking to pour into the lives of others.

It was during my teen years that I reconnected again with the Faith Mission when God sent Andrew Porter and Jonathan Bennett to serve in northern Ontario. Through them, I was able to attend camps and Youth Leadership Training that encouraged me and strengthen my faith.

At the age of seventeen, my dad died of cancer and while many would consider that a tragedy, God used it in my life to draw me closer to Him. I realized that without Christ my life had no meaning or purpose and that no matter what happened I would be all right so long as I had Him.

My plans for my life began to change. I no longer had a desire to further my education in any subject other than God's Word, so I enrolled in Briercrest Bible school. I had a sincere longing to know God's will and serve Him wherever He wanted me to go.

After many years and much prayer, God directed me to the Faith Mission. I joined the Mission when I was twenty-three years old and in the fall of 2007 headed to Quebec to work alongside Jennifer Katchikian (formerly Moldovan). While in the Mission, I was able to reconnect with Hester at one of our Ladies' Retreats. I was so encouraged as she shared that she had always had a heart to come to Quebec on a permanent basis. Instead of sending Hester, the Lord used her to lead a little girl to the Lord who would come one day and serve in her place.

That was ten years ago, and I can hardly believe all that God has led me to and by His grace, brought me through. The majority of ministry has been with children and youth, but there have been other opportunities opened up with adults also. There have been many challenges and tears, but there has also been great joy as I have seen God working in lives during these first years working in the Mission.

Jen and I often recognized the need for a man to come and work with the young people we were serving. God answered that prayer in Robin Perron, my husband. We were married in September 2014, and now we serve the Lord together with our little boy, Caleb.

We are privileged to serve the Lord and to teach His precious Word together. In the last few years, God directed us to start a Youth Leadership Training program here in Quebec. It has been exciting to see young people with a desire to know Christ more. These truly are exciting days.

We don't know what the future holds, but we look forward to continuing to serve the Lord together and are excited to see all He has in store for us, our family, the local churches and this province of Quebec.

Chapter 28—Christ Alone

Robin and Debra share several anecdotes from their time in Quebec:

One evening at the youth group, one of our young girls had invited a friend to attend. This particular boy was not from a Christian home, although his grandmother was a believer. He came with a lot of baggage as he faced many challenges due to several physical and behavioural conditions. For a long time, it was hard just to keep his attention during our Bible study times. As time went on, it became apparent that God was working in this young man's heart. He became the most attentive youth and had so many questions.

After a few years, this young man gave his heart to the Lord. He came to the youth group and pleaded with us to pray for his family, knowing that they were not saved. On one occasion, he came and told us that he had sold all of his video games because he was being convicted of the time he was spending playing with them instead of time for the Lord. It is in moments such as these that we are reminded why we have been called to serve—to have lives transformed by the Gospel and see Christ glorified! Praise God that He is in the business of saving and changing lives.

One of the areas where I have seen the least amount of fruit has been in children's ministry. As I look back on many years of teaching God's Word to children, I am encouraged in remembering God's promise in that His Word will accomplish the purpose for which He has sent it. I have not seen many children come to the Lord, but I have most definitely seen God at work in young lives.

A young boy who attended a kids' program had no Bible background at all. He was known in his school for being one of the most disruptive kids and was always in trouble. I admit that he was a bit of a handful to control, but something happened during the Bible lesson so that he became the most focused and attentive little boy present.

In those lessons, we were studying the life of Elijah, and during one of the stories, he began to shout out that the idols people were following were not the one true God. I will always have the image in my mind of this boy being upset and shouting out that there is only one God.

I haven't seen that boy in years and have no idea where he is now or what he even remembers from the Bible. What I do know is that he was taught the truth of God's Word and that God will use His Word to accomplish His purpose. This assurance gives me such hope that one day this boy might turn to Christ as he is reminded of the truth he learned.

It is a blessing and encouragement when we see young people seeking God's will for their lives. One particular girl who had chosen a career path many years earlier came and asked us to pray that God would make it very clear the direction in which He wanted her to go. She was willing to lay aside her plans if God had something else for her. May we see more young people willing to follow Christ wherever He may lead.

One particular young man shared how through reading God's Word he had become convicted of a particular sin in his life that he hadn't even realized was a sin. While he struggled and wrestled to gain victory over this sin, it was so encouraging to watch him striving to be obedient to Christ and honour Him with every part of his being.

CHAPTER 29

Growing Up and Going Out

The late Dr. Adrian Rogers of Bellevue Baptist Church in Memphis, Tennessee, said, "The most powerful and influential people on earth are Christian parents." The influence of Laura-Anne Drake's Christian home and her early association with the Faith Mission workers and camps helped shaped her life. Their spiritual input finally resulted in Laura-Anne joining the Mission in 2011. Here she testifies of how God has led and blessed her:

> Hi! I serve with the Faith Mission in Eastern Ontario. People often ask me how I got involved with the Faith Mission (in Canada). There is a sense in which I "grew up" with the Faith Mission in this great land. Let me explain.
>
> I had the privilege and blessing to be born into a Christian Family in Northern Ontario, where I gave my heart to the Lord at a young age. As a family, we attended Thornloe Crossroads Baptist Church; a church with which The Faith Mission has long associations. The pastor at that time had been saved at a children's meeting that had been led by former Faith Mission worker, Pearl White. I also fondly remember Brenda Thiessen and Ann Haliburton conducting Vacation Bible Schools in our Church.
>
> I remember that when I was fourteen years old, my

mother asked me if I wanted to spend my March break at a leadership camp down at the Faith Mission Centre in Campbellville. Although I agreed to go, I don't recall exactly what my expectations were for the week. However, I remember it was quite intensive, probably a little too much so, for the fourteen-year-old me. Nevertheless, I do remember a few things that were taught. One lesson was that it is always good to start your day with God and end it again with Him. I began to practice that on and off as a teenager and now it is something I implement today.

That following summer Andrew and Melissa Porter were holding a kids' camp in King Kirkland, Ontario. They were having a hard time finding a female counsellor, so they gave me a call a few weeks before camp. I was excited to help for I had always enjoyed camp, but I was also extremely nervous about being a counsellor. I told God that if he wanted me to do this, He would have to help me because I had no idea what I was doing. That week I knew God's help in a great way as He gave me wisdom when I led the cabin devotions and interacted with the kids. After that, I fell in love with the camp up there.

My fourteenth year marked the beginning of my spiritual "growing up" with the Faith Mission. Not only had I heard the stories of Pearl White and how she greatly influenced many for the Lord at my home church. I was now beginning to experience workers of the Faith Mission influencing me and spurring me on to "grow up" in the Lord.

The following year I went to the Youth Leadership Training (YLT) and helped at the camp up north. In my sixteenth year, I attended YLT again, this time in Napanee, Ontario. I remember it so clearly; I was sitting in a chair in the upstairs of the church where we were staying when Glenn Deane handed me a summer application. I knew at that

Chapter 29—Growing Up and Going Out

moment that God wanted me to spend my summer alongside a full-time Faith Mission worker, telling children about His plan of salvation. I was frightened as I knew it would mean that this shy, timid, young teenager would have to speak in front of people. I had known God's help in the past, and I told God again, "If You want me to do this You will have to help me."

That summer John Bennett placed me with Emma Glover in Napanee Ontario. One summer in Napanee turned into two. Little did I know that the house on Ginger Street would one day become home. Throughout those two summers, I experienced so much growth in my life. With God's grace I was able to stand up in front of kids and tell the Bible stories, lead quizzes and memory verses. God proved to me time and time again that He was my strong tower and when I trusted Him He could give strength to this shy and timid girl so she would have the boldness to talk to and in front of people. I remember clearly seeing God move at a week of camp meetings and thinking, "I can do nothing else with my life but serve Him in whatever way He wants me to."

After high school, I attended Nipawin Bible College, from which I received a Christian Ministry Diploma. During my time there I was praying that God would show me what the next step in my life would be. After Bible college, I returned home and started working at cleaning rooms in a hotel. I did not mind the work but knew God had something else in store for me.

About May of that year, I received an email from John Bennett asking me to spend the summer working with the Faith Mission. I remember thinking, "I'm very discontent right now; I loved my summers with the mission. This could be the perfect out. I can get this job back if I really want it in the fall."

That July I packed my bags and headed down to St. Thomas to work with Cheryl Mitchel. I can recall lying on the bed in the spare room reading my Bible. As I read, a few verses jumped out at me and in that moment I knew God was calling me to the work of the Faith Mission (in Canada).

However, instead of pursuing this, I went home and got another job. I fought against what God had clearly told me to do. I eventually became completely miserable and knew God was showing me that if I did not follow His specific will for my life, I would be miserable for the rest of my days. I applied to the Faith Mission at the end of August and entered into the work on October 1st, 2011.

My work with the Mission continues to be a constant "growth" experience. Over the last five and a half years, I have been stretched and challenged beyond what I thought was possible. I have seen God work and move in my life, and among the people I serve, as I chose daily to trust Him. Just like God has used Faith Mission workers to help me "grow up in the Lord," I pray that God will use me in the same way.

CHAPTER 30

Parental Channels

There is no doubt that the encouragement and wisdom imparted by Christian parents echoes in eternity. Just as young Timothy learned the Scriptures from his mother Eunice and grandmother Lois, and became a great servant of God, so the founder of the Faith Mission, John George Govan, was also the product of a godly home and praying parents.

God's work everywhere has been blessed by praying moms and dads who not only prayed their sons and daughters into the Kingdom of God but also out into God's work. That certainly was the case with many Faith Mission workers over the decades. Margaret Roberts is serving God today because of this same pattern.

> *I was born into a Christian home and from an early age had a full understanding of who Jesus Christ is and the sacrifice He had made for me. I am glad that I gave my heart and life to Christ as a young girl. Since my grandparents knew the purpose and vision of the Faith Mission, I was sent to the Faith Mission camps in Campbellville for several years. Those weeks greatly impacted my childhood and I remember never wanting camp to end. The rides back home were often filled with singing the camp songs and sharing stories with my mom and dad.*

When I was a teenager, I attended Youth Leadership Training over the March break—a week that is meant for those serious in their walk with God and gives them the opportunity to do outreach. That week profoundly impacted me as I experienced God in a way I hadn't before: at one point I so yearned for God and to serve Him. Little did we know it, but the week I attended YLT was the same week one of my future co-workers attended! I have found that the Lord certainly has a sense of humour!

Unfortunately, the change of heart didn't last very long for I was soon "swept up" into the life of high school, where I was introduced to new ideas, perspectives, and religions. This was the start of a time of trial for me, and I walked away from the Lord for a while. Many were praying for me at that point, and I have no doubt that my life was touched by the influence of their prayers.

When I was sixteen years old, I realized my grave mistake and recommitted myself to live for God. Not long after, my dad left my mom and me, but thankfully, that time of trial strengthened my relationship with God as I came to see Him not just as a Divine Being but also as a Heavenly Father.

After I had graduated high school, I began studying at Tyndale University College and Seminary in Toronto. Once I completed my first year, I started looking for summer work. For some reason, that can only be credited to the Lord, the Faith Mission (in Canada) came to my mind. Consequently, I was placed to work with Brenda Thiessen as a camp counsellor. Needless to say, that summer was instrumental in developing my relationship with God and teaching me leadership and teaching skills.

After that first summer, I was given a ride home by a Faith Mission worker. During the trip, I remember saying to

Chapter 30—Parental Channels

her that I wondered if God was calling me to be full-time with the Mission. However, once I began school again that thought quickly left me and, even though I returned to camp the next summer, I began to think there was no way I could be a full-time worker in the Faith Mission. As a result, for four out of five years, I wrestled with God and His calling on me to join the Faith Mission (in Canada).

At the end of my fourth year of university, I went on a trip with the Faith Mission to work in Southern Ireland and then I was back at the Campbellville Centre for a month. I also engaged in "maintenance work" at the campgrounds and helped in the annual "Thirsting for God conference."

Because of all these meetings, I was not only surrounded by Faith Mission workers, but their faith and dependence on God greatly impacted me. Once the conference was over, I found myself alone, pouring out my fears and concerns to God regarding the implications of joining the Faith Mission. In response, God gave me a verse in Deuteronomy 31:8: "The Lord is the One who will go before you. He will be with you; He will not leave you or forsake you. Do not be afraid or discouraged." *Once I received that verse, I knew that I needed to stop wrestling with God and surrender my will and fears over to Him.*

By the next summer, I officially became a full-time Faith Mission worker. Since then, I have repeatedly witnessed God's faithfulness and have been drawn into a deeper relationship with Him, for which I am thankful. He said, "Be satisfied with what you have, for He Himself has said, 'I will never leave you or forsake you'" *(Hebrews 13:5).*

CHAPTER 31

Their Labour of Love

Gospel ministry is not the monopoly of one person or group. Paul thanked the Christians at Philippi for their *"fellowship in the Gospel from the first day until now"* even though he was languishing in a Roman jail. Before being imprisoned, he wrote to the Christians in Rome and on the final page of his letter he mentioned more than thirty names. What is more important than the names are the verbs he used to describe how they *succoured* him, *laid down their necks* for him, *bestowed much labour* upon him, and on it goes. Even in the ministry of our Lord, we read of the Galilean ladies who followed Him to minister to Him.

The workers of the Faith Mission are filled with deep gratitude for the numerous friends who have ministered to them in numerous ways throughout its history. Space would not allow to mention them all, but we are assured that a record is made in Heaven and they will not lose their reward. The best commendation to them is what the writer to the Hebrews penned, *"God is not unrighteous to forget your work and labour of love, which you have shewed toward His name, in that you have ministered to the saints, and do minister"* (Hebrews 6:10).

Several of these helpers reminisce about their involvement with the Faith Mission (in Canada).

Isabel Minnett from Northern Ontario has been a faithful friend and helper of the Faith Mission. She recalls her vivid memories of former years:

Every fall when the Canada geese passed overhead on their annual trip to the south, our thoughts turn to Faith Mission. As well as signalling the advent of winter, we knew in earlier years that the flight of the geese was time for faithful mission workers to travel north. With their arrival, we felt a surge of excitement that these visitors always brought, but this was different.

Hosting the Workers

My husband Wayne's first memory of those days is when Harold Lund arrived. Harold stayed at his parents' home and held services in the nearby one-room school. That was the beginning of many years of hosting Faith Mission workers.

Pearl White came after that, and she became an icon, arriving year after year in her trusty Plymouth station wagon. She had loaded that vehicle beyond capacity with the latest audio visual aids: large story telling books, flannel graphs, projectors, and cassette tape player. Her paraphernalia changed as technology advanced. Winter was much harsher than what we have now—there were many storms with driving winds that created deep snowdrifts. This resulted in the side roads often being under several feet of snow. It always seemed to happen just when Pearl needed to get through for a meeting in a cold schoolroom somewhere in that district.

Pearl was a storyteller par excellence but as a driver? She gave a whole new meaning to the "Faith" part of "Faith Mission." She would pray for safe travels then set off, undaunted, through any eventuality, meanwhile patting the dashboard and encouraging "Betsy" (I think that was the

Chapter 31—Their Labour of Love

car's given name) to plough on through the snowdrifts. Perhaps some shovelling or a push was needed. Maybe she was late once in a while, but we do not recall a time when a meeting was cancelled.

Pearl stayed with me while I was teaching in Larder Lake. A few years later we were able to host the workers in our own home after we were married. We were so privileged to have her and other missionaries to visit the schools where we were teaching.

Some years later, we were asked to take responsibility for the funeral of a seventeen-year-old former student. This was not our usual assignment, so we called Pearl. She readily accessed her little record book in which she documented all the professions of faith, and to our comfort, she read out this little girl's name and the date of her conversion. What a help this was to us in the difficult days that followed.

Other Workers

Hester Dougan joined Pearl, and that also was an unqualified pleasure. Later, Hester came alone or with other Faith Mission workers; what fun times we had during those weeks. Today we cherish Hester and Ted's (Hester's husband, Ted Rendall) friendship to this day. Ann Hallyburton, Joyce Harrison, and Pat McMullen also came to our area. I know that many other workers accompanied these "old faithfuls" and we remember them well.

I treasure a little green and white "Irish" dress that Pat lovingly hand-stitched and sent to us on the birth of our first daughter. We have always admired the cheerful ministry rendered by these servants. It cannot be easy moving from home to home, and often, as in our case, having to blend into a busy *family with accommodations that were much less than luxurious, let alone private.*

Much has changed: access to children in a school setting is limited; technology has developed; the Faith Mission dress code of a blue suit and jaunty blue hat has disappeared. We have our very own Faith Mission workers, the Hardwicks, stationed nearby at King Kirkland, much to the area's benefit. However, these past workers are an integral part of our personal and corporate histories in Northern Ontario. Who knows the eternal extent of their outreach? And still, when the geese fly south, we relive those pleasant memories.

※ ※ ※ ※ ※

Pastor Steve Crosby, the Senior Pastor of the Good Shepherd Church in Englehart, Ontario, writes of his appreciation for the Faith Mission's multi-faceted influence:

For nearly a quarter of a century, the Faith Mission's work in Canada has influenced our lives from Southern Ontario to Northeastern Ontario. Their availability to our churches and people, as well as their ability to intercept the routine with deeper challenges, has left us nourished and encouraged in the faith.

We often gathered folks together for mini-conferences and special speakers in Beamsville, Ontario, where the Word was preached and introspection brought us to Spirit-led conviction. Whatever our theme might be, from Mission Conference to Revival Meeting, the Faith Mission fulfilled the mandate of Christ.

I walked the rooms of the Campbellville Retreat and Conference Centre, where Director John Bennett and the excellent workers accepted in this pile of youth and children

Chapter 31—Their Labour of Love

for a weekend of Gospel ministry. It was touching, knowing that some of the children who were well known to me were coming from lives of poverty and neglect. In conversations with them, they have never forgotten the commitments they made on this retreat and the sheer encouragement it was to them as they struggled in their walk of faith.

Our local church in the Englehart, Ontario area was blessed by the Faith Mission workers as we began an annual DVBS and found out that the Mission supplied a fantastic curriculum. The Hardwick family worked hard, driving down from Kirkland Lake daily to minister to our children, teaching them Bible, mission stories, and memory verses. They led in games, music and relationship building, all of it centred on Christ. We greatly appreciate their ministry to our local church.

That being said, twice now, I have sat in my church office when the Hardwicks have made their drive down to seek to encourage us in our ministry. Their first phone call to us was to state the fact that they wanted to encourage pastors and churches directly. I have had the privilege of being influenced by the Faith Mission on various levels, and I know and trust that this relationship will continue.

In their ministry, they never stand aloof. You make lifelong friendships with all of their workers. The Faith Mission is a local-body blessing that I pray will expand and encourage many more churches in the years to come. They are marked by faithfulness and consistency in their relationship with the Lord, in their giving of His Word, and in the relationships they build along the way

We thank God for you every time we hear of your work.

Rev. Herb Van Essen, Pastor of Wilton Church in Wilton, Ontario, expressed his appreciation for Laura-Anne Drake and Margaret Roberts, Faith Mission workers who have worked with the local church in Wilton.

> *We at Wilton Church thank the Lord for the ministry of the Faith Mission through Laura-Anne and Margaret in providing ministry to both children and teens in our community. If it weren't for their dedication and hard work each week, we would no doubt not have this opportunity since our congregation is made up of mostly senior citizens.*
>
> *For most of these children and teens, the work of Faith Mission is the only "church" that they are exposed to. We believe that the seed planting of the Word of God and His love demonstrated through Laura-Anne and Margaret will in time reap a harvest for the Kingdom.*
>
> *Watching these young ladies commit their time and energies, I am truly thankful that they keep persevering in their work. The Kids Club time can be especially challenging, and in the evening where only one or two children show up, they seem never to be discouraged.*
>
> *We trust that our future of working together will continue to be a positive experience for all.*

Chapter 32

I Met the Saviour

The greatest evidence of the power of the Gospel is a transformed life. Every conversion is a miracle whereby the sinner is born again by the Holy Spirit to a new life in Christ, and God makes that person a brand new creature. For every Christian, God has a purpose in living. The greatest joy of the Christian's life is discovering, doing, and delighting in the will of God.

Through the ministry of Faith Mission workers, numerous people have been led to faith in Christ and then nurtured in that faith and encouraged to seek God's blessing on their surrendered lives.

Johnny Richards serves God and country in the Canadian Navy, and God is using him to speak to his fellow Navy personnel. Here is Johnny's testimony:

> *I was raised in a Christian family. We did the usual things expected from Christian families, and sometimes more; we always went to church, Bible studies, VBSs, Sunday school, youth groups and their annual retreats to various Christian camps, etc. I started going to Faith Mission events at a very young age. On top of all that, my parents homeschooled me and gave me a special Christian and biblically based curriculum. We, therefore, grew up with other Christian families within our local home-school group.*

Though I couldn't see it at the time, God had poured blessing upon blessing on me. As I grew older, I began to realize just how much I didn't deserve His blessings. One day it suddenly hit me like a ton of bricks that He had not only blessed me with such an ideal and fortunate childhood but also, He had died for me and took the punishment for my sins, sins He did not commit. It made no sense to me.

I accepted Jesus into my heart at the age of four and was baptized on December 7, 2008 at Grace Baptist Church. However, I remember I did this partly because of the "peer pressure" I had felt from without, rather than from God's calling within—everyone else was doing it, so I did it too. But thinking myself to be "righteous," I didn't sincerely repent of my sin and accept God's forgiveness. I figured I was "good enough."

I was so proud and self-righteous. Surrender to God was not what I wanted. I tried to stop sinning in my own strength, and maybe I took a step or two forward, but each time, I'd fall right back to the start. I wasn't able and became immensely depressed. Things got so bad that I began to think, What on earth am I doing here? What's happened to me? *I shuddered to realize just how desperately wicked I was, yet with all my strength I could not just stop sinning as if sin had an off switch.*

Fast forward a little to the beginning of 2013 when I went to the Faith Mission's Snow Camp, as I usually did twice a year. On the last day of camp, I was invited to the Youth Leadership Training Weekend during March break. I was told to pray about it, so I did. Later at home, I realized the camp conflicted with the day I had planned to go snowboarding with my friends, so I tried to brush it off since snowboarding was one of my most favourite activities in all the world and only got to do it once or twice a year. However, God made it clear to me that He wanted me to go to the Faith Mission's weekend.

Chapter 32—I Met the Saviour

The snowboard trip was cancelled, which left me no excuse, and for this, I am now extremely thankful. Had I gone snowboarding and rejected God, who knows where I would be today? I would probably still be a slave to my sin.

I went to the Youth Leadership Training, and I can put it no plainer than to say that God made Himself clear to me. I was conscious of His presence every waking second—in the study sessions, prayer times, and in the lives of nearly everyone around me, albeit not my own. He was there, waiting for me to open the door of my heart and life to let Him in. Each night the campers prayed together, and each night I battled with God. I prayed silently while numerous people prayed out loud. I told myself each night that I would pray out loud too. I felt like I had to do something to show that I wasn't just faking my walk with God, but I retained a heart of stone and a rebellious will so that I couldn't let go or open my heart's door.

God really humbled me by using a young, handicapped girl who prayed every single night. I thought, If she could do it, why can't I? *I was extremely jealous of the people who prayed and their apparent relationship with God. I admired the fire they had for God in their hearts, and I wanted that.*

On the last night, I knew I had to pray if I wanted to maintain the charade. However, God had something else in store. That evening we didn't pray as we normally had done on other nights. We bowed our heads while Mr. Bennett prayed out loud, challenging us to surrender our lives and our wills to God. He said something like, "It's not by our strength, but God's."

I took that to heart, and I didn't go to sleep that night until I got right with God. I prayed for a long time, asking for His forgiveness for sins I hate to even think about. I cried out to God, and said, "Here's me."

From that day on, I determined that God would have His way with me. However, old habits die hard. The things I wanted to do, I didn't, and the things I didn't want to do, I did. I needed to do away with the old me and become accountable to someone, but I initially neglected doing this because of my shame. Again, I wanted to look like I had everything under control.

When I was at my lowest point and feeling furthest from God, I turned to His Word, searching for answers. On May 2, 2014, I opened my Bible to Proverbs 28:13-14: "He that covereth his sins shall not prosper: but whoso confesseth and forsaketh them shall have mercy. Happy is the man that feareth always: but he that hardeneth his heart shall fall into mischief."

Immediately, I felt convicted. I knew God was challenging me, calling me and that it wasn't too late. I knew what I had to do; it was crystal clear: confess and forsake my sins; lay them at the foot of the cross, no matter the shame or the cost. So I confessed my sins unto God and my mother. That was one of the hardest things I've ever had to do, but definitely the best. Finally, I was free. By surrendering my will to God and letting Him take control, forsaking my sin became easier. I finally felt I was truly born again. God confirmed this in my life by completely changing my desires. I was hungry for God's Word and His will in my life; praying and reading my Bible were no longer chores. The more I prayed and read, the more I wanted. Previously, my appetite was my god. Now, God is my appetite!

Before His grace reached and saved me, I was too proud and didn't accept God's forgiveness. When He humbled me I began to think, "How could He use someone like me? I'm incompetent in every way…surely He's got the wrong man."

Chapter 32—I Met the Saviour

It was then that God reminded me what He had done through the reluctant Jeremiah, the hesitant Moses, the fearful Gideon, and young David. God was not looking for someone's capability, but rather their availability. He is faithful to enable those who are available and put their trust in Him.

* * * * *

Lea Haist is another friend of the Faith Mission who offers her testimony:

Although I was born out of wedlock and raised in a non-Christian home, I loved my parents, despite their drinking, fighting, cursing and hatred. As a child, I was baptized and confirmed in the Anglican Church, but I knew only a little about Jesus and did not have a personal relationship with Him.

Ross and I were married when I was twenty. I am grateful that God blessed me with such a wonderful and loving husband. He also blessed our home with two wonderful sons. We attended church occasionally, but we lived our lives without God.

In 1989 my stepfather and brother died of cancer, and I feared the thought of them going to Hell. For twelve years I was restless and often cried out, "God, what do you want from me?" The Lord was speaking to me for I realized there was "something" missing in my life.

One day, through tears, I saw a sign outside a church which read: "Calvary Baptist Church, Burlington, Bible Study, Wednesday Evening." I mistakenly thought I couldn't go to a Baptist Church. But God helped me to go to the church and meet the Youth Pastor. As I wept, he listened to me. He gave me a Bible with an invitation to return to the church. I did go back and cried during Bible study and church service.

Everything in that church, the message, the words and the songs, touched my heart.

On April 14th, 2004, John and Isabel Bennett, from the Faith Mission in Campbellville, came to our church Missions Conference, where John spoke. At the end of his message, he gave an altar call. That day, again with tears streaming down my face, I went forward and accepted Christ into my life.

I began to pray specifically for my husband's salvation and waited for him to accept Christ. I learned that this would have to be in God's time, so I lived as Christ enabled me, kept on praying and let the Lord do the rest. Not long after this, Ross accepted Christ into his life, and soon my oldest son, Brock, also received salvation. I am so thankful for God's faithfulness.

In the spring of 2005, after a representative from Careforce International came to our church, I sponsored a girl from the Dominican Republic. Later, I received an invitation to be part of a short-term missions trip to that country. My church family blessed me by funding the trip. I saw God's love at work through Careforce, and several times that week I met girls whom I sponsor. That trip changed me. I have learned so much about myself, and instead of murmuring, I must trust in the Lord.

I cannot change a culture, but I can serve and spread God's love. I have also learned the importance of prayer and thanksgiving. I thank God every day for His love, kindness, faithfulness, mercy, and for His grace in my trials. I have learned how patient our God is. He waited patiently for me for fifty-seven years. Now I worship Him with gladness, and I sing His praise with joy in my heart. Tears continue to flow, tears for the lost and tears of joy.

Chapter 32—I Met the Saviour

Iris Berry shares:

I grew up in in a Catholic family in Clontarff, Dublin. I knew there was something missing in my religion. I came to Canada when I was in my early twenties, and it was here, visiting different churches throughout Eastern Ontario, that I first learned about the Faith Mission (in Canada). I attended Calvary Pentecostal Church for some time. It was there one night that I heard a few testimonies from Faith Mission workers. Like me, some of them had also grown up in Catholic homes, but their lives were different. I saw in them a passion for God, and for people. They loved the Lord and were not afraid to say so. Their faith in Jesus Christ impacted me.

After I had come to know Jesus as my Saviour, I realized that God was calling me into kids' ministry and that I needed to get "out of my comfort zone." The testimonies and faith of those Mission workers have made a lasting impression on me. Today, I am connected to Faith Mission workers in Napanee, Ontario, where I help with their monthly Adorned Ladies' meeting.

CHAPTER 33

A Heart Cry for Revival

Rev. Jacques Nadeau is Senior Pastor of Newcastle Fellowship Baptist Church, Ontario. Under his ministry, God has greatly blessed the church, and as a result, many new families have been added to the congregation. Pastor Nadeau shares the burden of all Faith Mission workers for a nationwide revival in Canada. During most of his fourteen years at the Newcastle Fellowship Baptist Church, he has annually hosted the Faith Mission's "Thirsting for God Conferences."

Pastor Nadeau wrote the following:

According to a sidebar in Christian History *magazine, spiritual awakenings or revivals, whether in biblical history or in Church history, often manifest very similar patterns that are strikingly the same. Usually, the following spiritual elements are always present:*

Awakenings are often preceded by a time of spiritual depression, moral apathy, and gross sin, in which a majority of nominal Christians are hardly any different from the members of secular society, and the Churches seem to be asleep.

An individual, or a small group of God's people, become so conscious of their sin and of their backslidden condition that they vow to forsake anything and everything, that's displeasing to God in their lives, or that they know would grieve the Holy Spirit.

As some believers begin to yearn for a manifestation of God's divine presence and power, a leader or leaders arise, with great spiritual insight into the causes and remedies of the problem. A new awareness of the holy and pure character of God begins to consume and grip the people of God. This fills them with a holy fear of God, and a passion to live the kind of lives that are pleasing in His sight.

The awakening of believers begins to occur; many Christians begin to understand and take part in a much more real and deeper spiritual life. Sinners are often converted to the Lord Jesus Christ because of the very strong sense of the Presence of the Spirit of God among His people.

An awakening or revival is often the very means that God uses to prepare and strengthen His people for the days of evil that are fast approaching.

Dr. Stephen Olford said, "A revival is an invasion from Heaven that brings us a conscious awareness of God." Robert Coleman said, "Revival is that sovereign work of God in which He visits His own people, restoring and releasing them into the fullness of His blessing." James A. Stewart said, "Revival is the people of God living in the power of an ungrieved and unquenched Holy Spirit." Brian Edwards said, "In revival, the minds of the people are concentrated upon the things of eternity, and there's an awareness that nothing else really matters."

I have become convinced, beyond any shadow of doubt, that a time of revival and spiritual renewal among the people of God is what the Church in North America so desperately needs in this current day. We need to be living in the power of an ungrieved and unquenched Holy Spirit; our faces need to

Chapter 33—A Heart Cry for Revival

grow pale, and we need to drop down to our knees and fall prostrate to the floor, as one believer goes to another believer and confesses wrong feelings towards one another, and as the sins of pride, anger, bitterness, envy, jealousy, lust, hatred, greed, impurity, dissension, division, strife, and rivalries are not only openly confessed to Jesus Christ, but also sincerely forsaken and renounced.

We need to become so conscious of our sin and so aware of the holy and pure character of our God and of the call of the Gospel and of the Cross that we would vow to forsake "anything and everything" that's displeasing to God and that would violate His holy will, as revealed to us in Holy Scripture.

Samuel Stevenson said it so well when he penned the words to the following poem:

> A city full of churches, great preachers, lettered men;
> Grand music, choirs and organs, if all these fail, what then?
> Good workers, eager, earnest, who labor hour by hour;
> But where, Oh, where, my brother, is God's almighty power?
>
> Refinement, education, they want the very best;
> Their plans and schemes are perfect; they give themselves no rest.
> They get the best of talent, they try their uttermost,
> But what they need, my dear brother, is God the Holy Ghost.
>
> We may spend time and money, and preach from wisdom's lore,
> But education only will keep God's people poor.
> God wants not worldly wisdom, He seeks no smile to win;
> But what is needed, oh, my brother, is that we deal with sin.
>
> It is the Holy Spirit, who quickeneth the soul.
> God will not take man-worship, nor bow to man's control.
> No human innovation, no skill or worldly art,
> Can give a true repentance, or break the sinner's heart.

We may have human wisdom, grand singing, great success.
There may be fine equipment, but these things do not bless.
God wants a pure, clean vessel, anointed lips and true;
A man filled with His Spirit, to speak His message through.

Great God, revive us truly, and keep us every day,
That men may all acknowledge, "We live just as we pray."
The Lord's hand is not shortened, He still delights to bless
If we depart from evil, and all our sins confess!

We need revival; we so desperately need a visitation from God. In the fourteen years that I have been the pastor of Newcastle Fellowship Baptist Church, this has been, and continues to be, the cry of my heart: "Father, make us a people of prayer, purity and passion!"

Almost every year, the Faith Mission comes alongside us, in this great unrelenting burden of our souls, as we have hosted many "Thirsting for God" Bible conferences, and as we have sought the Lord together for the transforming work of His Spirit in our nation in such a way that we have never known it before.

I count it a privilege to link arms with men like John Bennett, and all the staff of the Faith Mission, as we continue to pursue our God for a mighty outpouring of His grace and power that will literally shake the foundations of His Church!

Invade us, Father, with Your divine presence, as we humbly bow our knees before You, and turn our faces, and not our backs, to your divine will.

CHAPTER 34

Prayer, Evangelism, and Revival

John Bennett explains that three words sum up the primary emphasis of the Faith Mission's ministry in Canada: *prayer, evangelism,* and *revival.*

PRAYER

Tracing the Mission's history back to those early days in Glasgow, Scotland, when God was moulding a young business man who later became the founder of the Mission, we can see how prayer became a major component in the life of the Mission. John George Govan and his fellow labourers at the Water Street Mission spent whole nights and full days in prayer. They knew what it was to battle through to Heaven during hours of waiting on God. They recognized that if victory were to be secured, it would only be accomplished on their knees before God. Later, when he and others went from community to community conducting evangelistic missions, a battle for souls often raged. Their only recourse was to fall before God in earnest believing prayer. Story after story could be told of the great battles fought in prayer and the glorious victories accomplished for the glory of God.

It was in answer to the prayers of some concerned Christians in Toronto that the Faith Mission came to Canada. Those early evangelists and local believers waited on God, pleaded for the salvation of souls and spent many hours in prayer. Their lives and work should make us blush when we realize how little we know of such prevailing prayer. They were not willing to settle for defeat or less than God's best. They held on in prayer until God broke through. I wonder what would happen today if the church were to reinstate half nights and whole nights of prayer into the monthly schedule. God's people need to take His promises seriously and plead them before God's throne expecting an answer from heaven.

One of the great blessings the Faith Mission enjoys is that most of its supporters are praying people and are committed to their weekly church prayer meetings. They tell us that they pray for the Mission daily, often mentioning each worker by name. For almost one hundred and thirty years, the Prayer Union movement, which was started by Mr. Govan, has continued to the present time. At the weekly or monthly Prayer Union, people from different churches meet to pray for the Faith Mission, the local church and revival. We thank God for those who meet in Canada and long to see this number multiply. Someone has said, "God does nothing without prayer and everything with it."

D.L. Moody said, "Those who have left the deepest impression on this sin cursed world have been men and women of prayer."

Northern Ireland evangelist, J. Edwin Orr, wrote, "Every revival has its earthly origin in prayer...there has never been a revival that did not start in united prayer."

Chapter 34—Prayer, Evangelism, and Revival

At the Faith Mission, we can attest to the fact that every significant spiritual advance through the years can be traced back to prayer and praying people.

For five or six years, the Faith Mission (in Canada) led an annual week of prayer in a particular church. When God began to bless the pastor looked back over the years and declared, "I can trace every significant blessing that has come to this church back to those weeks of prayer."

Gerhard du Toit who, with his wife, Janice, directed the work in B.C. for some years, was greatly used of God in ministry and the development of the Faith Mission Centre in Surrey. He wrote in 1999,

> On the day of Pentecost there was only one sermon, but there were ten days of prayer after which three thousand souls were saved. In this century we invert the apostolic order and have ten days of preaching, mere scraps of time for prayer, and we have more often failed than succeeded in our effort to save souls.

Pastor Gordon Phillips said,

> Prayer and its efficacy in our lives is a mystery and a glory. It turns our hearts towards the Master of our souls. It probes our spirits. It leads to confession of sin. It puts us in touch with the infinite resources of our Heavenly Father. It inspires in us a longing for His glory and His salvation.

Brother and sister, as you read this account of what God has done, will you not dedicate yourself afresh to become a man or woman of prayer? Will you make it your business, where possible, to attend your regular church prayer meeting? Perhaps you would like to start a Faith Mission Prayer Union in your area if there is not one there already.

Evangelism

John George Govan famously said, "If the Faith Mission ceases to be a soul-saving agency it does not deserve to exist." Evangelism, the saving of souls, reaching the lost, rescuing men, women, boys and girls from a lost Hell, is at the heart of our entire ministry. The Faith Mission workers recognize that all have sinned, all are under the judgement and wrath of a Holy God, that no one can save him or herself, that the only means whereby a person can be saved and enter Heaven is by grace alone, through faith alone, in Jesus Christ alone.

In earlier years, evangelistic campaigns often lasted for many weeks. During those campaigns, Mission evangelists spent mornings in prayer and preparation, afternoons visiting every home, and then meetings in the evenings. Thrilling accounts of many of these campaigns have been recorded. In the archives, we can read reports of five, ten and sometimes thirty or more adults trusting the Saviour and many children seeking the Lord. More recently, churches have been reluctant to hold such prolonged series of evangelistic meetings. Today, church leadership is more likely to allocate a week or weekend for an evangelistic mission. Much of the evangelism carried out by the Faith Mission (in Canada) at present is either through regular clubs, special events, Christianity Explored courses, Bible studies, retreats, pulpit supply or street outreach. I share snippets from our December 1993 newsletter. These could be multiplied many times over.

> "Two girls professed faith in Christ and others raised their hands but did not testify."

> "Thirty-one responded…travelled 42,929 km."

> "The Discovery Club went well—six children professed."

Chapter 34—Prayer, Evangelism, and Revival

"There was such brokenness at the close that the whole congregation responded."

"There were ten children at the meeting, and four of them responded for salvation."

"...to see 250-300 people seeking God, some until around 2:00pm, just gave us a passion to see God work."

"The early morning prayer meetings were an inspiration. During the week we had thirteen adult services and two open sessions at Sunday schools. Eleven people responded for specific needs."

"A lady in a wheelchair asked someone to push her to the front. A man in his eighties was one of some older saints seeking God."

"We registered 59 kids here, three of whom trusted the Saviour."

"Times of prayer each evening and the half day of prayer on Thursday were precious times."

"It was thrilling to know that at least half of the forty campers trusted the Lord as Saviour."

"A text board and distribution of 400 tracts were a faithful witness."

"Every home in the area was visited."

"Over 130 children were registered, and at least three trusted the Saviour."

"...spoke to the high school students, three of whom came out for salvation."

We would love to see the vision for direct evangelism restored within the churches. It is as true today as when this hymn was written:

Untold millions are still untold,
Untold millions are outside the fold.
Who will tell them of Jesus love
And the Heavenly mansions awaiting above?
Jesus died on Calvary to save each one from sin.
Now He calls for you and me to go and bring them in,
For many untold millions are still untold
Untold millions are outside the fold.

Revival

The word revival *has been greatly misunderstood over the years. It has often been used to describe a series of meetings. People talk about having revival meetings. In most cases, revival is their aim, but not their experience. Within the history of the Faith Mission, God has privileged the work with times of revival. This happened when God came in unusual power into a community, causing His presence to invade the district. When Duncan Campbell described the revival in Scotland, he spoke of it as "a people saturated with God." The Puritans' definition of revival was "the manifest presence of God."*

The Faith Mission was blessed to be around in 1904 when the Welsh revival was at its height. Again, the Mission was active in the 1920s when God moved in power in Northern Ireland. During the late 1940s and early 1950s, God did such mighty things in Scotland where the Mission was working.

There was a touch of revival in Nova Scotia when Ken and Nellie Buchanan worked with the Mission in that area. For a period, the presence of God was so real in a particular community that strangers travelling through suddenly became convicted of their sin. At that time Ken went out into the bush to pray until he knew he had got through to God for the

Chapter 34—Prayer, Evangelism, and Revival

meeting. At the meetings, people were gripped by the power of God and arrested by His voice.

When travelling to speak at a Canadian Bible School Chapel in the 1990s, a Faith Mission worker felt such a burden that he had to pull over to the side of the road many times to pray before he got to the school. At the chapel service, he shared what was in his heart but did not feel anything extraordinary. When the chapel leader stood up to close the service and dismiss the students, a staff member suddenly stood up and brokenly confessed her sin and asked for forgiveness.

For the next number of hours, students were confessing sin and asking forgiveness from God and other people. Lunchtime passed, and the meeting continued. Only in the afternoon were the students dismissed. Later, some of them confessed that they had experienced a moment of revival in their hearts.

Duncan Campbell said that having been in revival spoiled him for anything less. The heart cry of every Faith Mission worker is for revival in Canada. They are convinced that nothing less than a God-sent revival will stem the downward tide that is sweeping this nation. 2 Chronicles 7:14 grips our hearts and stirs our souls: "If my people, which are called by my name, shall humble themselves, and pray, and seek my face, and turn from their wicked ways; then will I hear from heaven, and will forgive their sin, and will heal their land."

May God help us all to humble ourselves, *acknowledge our need, recognize our failure, and* pray consistent, persevering, believing prayer; seek God's face, *not willing just to say prayers, but to seek an audience with the King;* turn from our wicked ways, *true repentance, forsaking of sin;* and then God has promised to hear, heal and forgive.

CHAPTER 35

The Great Commission

Jesus came and said to them, *"All authority in Heaven and on Earth has been given to Me. Go therefore and make disciples of all nations, baptizing them in the name of the Father and of the Son and of the Holy Spirit, teaching them to observe all that I have commanded you. And behold I am with you always, to the end of the age"* (Matthew 28:18-20).

Revival in Canada

Long ago, brave John Cabot Northwest would go
Royal lands to gain, in Henry's reign.
Refugee, with fleur-de-lis, French Huguenot
'scaped tyrants blow, freedom to know.

All this mighty land of Canada,
Oh Canada, Yes Canada,
From the river and from sea to sea,
His dominion it shall be!

Newfoundland, Prince Edward Isle, Maritimes;
Quaint French Québec, Ontario,
Prairie range and foothills blue, the Cariboo;
Cold Artic space, these parts we know.

The Canadian Commission

Triune God, our fathers' God, come to my heart,
Bid sin depart, Thy life impart,
Mighty burning, cleansing Flame sweep through each part
From heart to heart, revival start.

—Hutcheson MacFarlane